T0370439

HEAR WHAT THE
SHADOWS REVEAL

Shawn Sellers & David Humphrey

authorHOUSE®

AuthorHouse™
1663 Liberty Drive
Bloomington, IN 47403
www.authorhouse.com
Phone: 833-262-8899

Published by AuthorHouse 06/13/2024

ISBN: 979-8-8230-2737-3 (sc)
ISBN: 979-8-8230-2738-0 (e)

Library of Congress Control Number: 2024910550

Print information available on the last page.

This book is printed on acid-free paper.

Contents

Hear What the Shadows Reveal

By Shawn Sellers & David Humphrey

In the darkened corners where whispers hide,
Voices from the shadows, secrets confide.
Whispers of the past, echoes of pain,
Revealing tales that drive the sane.
Mysteries shrouded in a cloak of night,
Unveiled by voices that long for light.
Secrets buried deep, yearning to break free,
Haunting the shadows, begging to be seen.
Listen closely to the secrets they share,
Stories of love, of loss, of despair.
Echoes of joy and echoes of sorrow,
Whispered in darkness, shaping tomorrow.
In the shadows lie truths long ignored,
Whispers of wisdom, of battles once roared.
Voices from the past calling our name,
Guiding us forward, never the same.
So heed the voices that linger unseen,
In the shadows, they dwell, where secrets convene.
Listen and learn from the tales they impart,
Voices from the shadows touching the heart.

Introduction

Hear What the Shadows Reveal

Welcome to the journey of a lifetime—a journey born from a bond that has withstood the tests of time and a shared dedication to unveiling the truths lurking in our world's shadows. As David Humphrey and I, Shawn Sellers, childhood friends and brothers in the Masonic order, we invite you to join us on a profound exploration fueled by over four decades of friendship and a combined experience of over 25 years in diverse professional fields.

Our paths diverged professionally, yet our shared mission remains steadfast: to expose the grim realities that plague our society, particularly the insidious crimes of human trafficking, Satanic Ritual Abuse (SRA), and the exploitation of the most vulnerable among us—our children.

Drawing from my background in Religious Studies and Special Education, alongside David's expertise as a business owner and law enforcement officer, we have unearthed a shared commitment to confronting these atrocities head-on. David's founding of the Alabama Alliance for Human Trafficking and Child Safety is a testament to our collective resolve. At the same time, my role as the organization's education director underscores our dedication to empowering communities through knowledge and awareness.

After years of bearing witness to the darkest aspects of humanity, we have come together to pen "Unveiling Darkness"—a chronicle that dives deep into the abyss of human trafficking, the agony of missing persons, the chilling realities of SRA, and the exploitation of innocent lives. Our book is not merely a recounting of facts but a call to arms, an urgent plea for action in the face of unfathomable injustice.

As you turn the pages of our book, we implore you to absorb its contents and heed its call—to stand alongside us in the fight against exploitation and abuse. Let our words be a catalyst for change, igniting a fire within you to advocate, educate, and protect those who cannot defend themselves.

May "Unveiling Darkness" inform and inspire, guiding you on a journey of enlightenment and empowerment. Together, let us illuminate the path forward, driven by the light of awareness and fueled by the collective power of action. Join us as we confront the shadows, daring to dream of a safer, more just world for all.

About ten years ago, I found myself standing at a crossroads. My marriage was faltering, and the weight of years spent immersed in paranormal research across the United States had left me weary and adrift. Seeking refuge in the comforting embrace of New Orleans, I hoped to rediscover clarity and purpose amidst its familiar streets.

During a weekend retreat, I joined a tour led by a longtime friend, only to find him absent, replaced by his assistant. As we lingered behind the cathedral, he regaled me with chilling accounts of a possible serial killer haunting the city. Tales of missing souls, some discovered bound in abandoned warehouses, stirred a deep unease within me. The eerie refrain, "No body, no crime," echoed in my mind, sparking a genuine curiosity.

Returning to my hotel, I plunged into research, unearthing a labyrinth of leads. Eager to share my discoveries, I confided in my friend David, who shared my intrigue. Over dinner, amid the restaurant's din, we found ourselves unexpectedly drawn into a conversation with a retired police officer and his elderly mother. Against the backdrop of an impending storm, their presence felt like more than luck.

As introductions unfolded, the retired officer revealed shocking revelations of a clandestine network entwined with law enforcement and occult rituals. His accounts of a harrowing ritualistic massacre left me speechless, grappling with the magnitude of what I had stumbled upon.

Reflecting on past encounters, I recognized a recurring theme of occult influence in the supernatural realm. Despite my intention to step back, the universe seemed to beckon me forward, unveiling a path fraught with mystery and peril.

In the following years, I dedicated myself to unraveling the tangled web of occult connections, drawing from my research and experiences. As I embark on chronicling these tales, I am driven to delve deeper into the shadows, illuminating the enigmatic forces at play.

Through sharing these stories, I hope to shed light on the obscure, weaving a tapestry of truth from the threads of the unknown. Indeed, this encounter with David was a pivotal moment that propelled us down this research path.

Shedding Light on the Underreported Reality of Child Sex Trafficking

In a world fraught with darkness, individuals like Shawn and David courageously embark on journeys to uncover the harrowing reality of child sex trafficking. Their exploration of this clandestine world often begins with a simple research project, which unveils shocking truths about trafficking rings operating even within their communities. Through their work, they illuminate the disturbing scale of the issue, emphasizing the urgent need for awareness, action, and justice.

The clandestine world of child sex trafficking remains one of the most insidious and pervasive forms of exploitation, inflicting devastating consequences on its victims. Despite conservative estimates suggesting that up to 500,000 children are trapped in sex trafficking daily, the true scope of this crime may far exceed 1.2 million. However, the shocking reality is that only 1% of cases are reported, often decades after the abuse occurs, presenting significant challenges for investigations and hindering the pursuit of justice. This paper delves into the complexities of unreported child sex trafficking, examining the factors contributing to underreporting and the profound implications for victims and society at large.

Child sex trafficking is a global epidemic, with millions of children falling victim to this heinous crime each year. Shocking statistics reveal the prevalence of trafficking rings operating across continents, exploiting vulnerable children for profit. Despite efforts to quantify the scale of the issue, a significant discrepancy exists between reported and unreported cases, making it challenging to assess the true extent of the problem accurately.

Numerous factors contribute to the underreporting of child sex trafficking cases, perpetuating a culture of silence and impunity. Fear and intimidation tactics employed by traffickers often silence victims, preventing them from seeking help or disclosing their abuse. Additionally, survivors face stigma and shame, further discouraging them from coming forward and seeking support. Moreover, a lack of trust in law enforcement and justice systems, coupled with barriers to accessing support services, creates additional hurdles for victims seeking assistance.

The underreporting of child sex trafficking has profound implications for victims and society as a whole. Prolonged trauma and psychological impact on survivors can have long-lasting effects, perpetuating cycles of abuse and exploitation. Furthermore, inadequate allocation of resources for prevention and intervention efforts hinders efforts to combat trafficking effectively. Society's complicity in allowing child sex trafficking to persist through silence and inaction further exacerbates the problem, perpetuating a cycle of victimization and impunity.

Addressing underreporting requires a multifaceted approach that focuses on strengthening victim support services, enhancing training and awareness among professionals, promoting community engagement, and advocating for policy changes. By prioritizing survivor-centered approaches, improving access to resources, and fostering collaboration among stakeholders, we can create a more supportive environment for victims and increase accountability for traffickers.

Shedding light on the underreported reality of child sex trafficking is essential for raising awareness, fostering action, and seeking justice for victims. By understanding the factors contributing to underreporting and its profound implications, we can work towards creating a society where exploitation and abuse are no longer tolerated and all children are protected from harm. Through collaborative efforts and unwavering commitment, we can strive toward a future where every child can live free from the shackles of trafficking and exploitation.

Recent revelations have shed light on the existence of the 'dark web' and its insidious role in facilitating illegal transactions, including human trafficking and exploitation. Using digital currency in platforms like Second Life for money laundering and transactions on the dark web has further compounded the challenges in combating these crimes. This paper explores the tactics employed by human traffickers, including the progression of victims from pornography to human bondage and drug manufacturing, as well as their role in recruiting younger girls into the sex trade. Additionally, it examines the long-term consequences of trafficking victims' exploitation and abuse, along with implications and recommendations for addressing these pressing issues.

The 'dark web' represents a hidden corner of the internet where illicit activities thrive, including the buying and selling of contraband, drugs, weapons, and even human beings. Its anonymity and encryption make it an ideal platform for traffickers to operate with impunity, facilitating transactions without fear of detection. Using digital currency, such as Bitcoin, in platforms like Second Life further complicates efforts to track and trace illegal transactions, providing traffickers a cloak of invisibility.

Human traffickers employ a variety of tactics to exploit and manipulate their victims, often preying on vulnerabilities and using coercion to maintain control. Victims are lured into the sex trade through false promises of employment, education, or a better life, only to find themselves trapped in a cycle of abuse and exploitation. The progression from pornography to human bondage and drug manufacturing underscores the ruthless nature of traffickers, who exploit their victims for profit at every opportunity. Additionally, victims may be coerced into recruiting younger girls into the sex trade, perpetuating the cycle of exploitation.

The long-term consequences of trafficking victims' exploitation and abuse are profound and far-reaching, extending beyond the immediate physical and psychological trauma. Survivors often struggle with complex trauma, PTSD, and a range of mental health issues, which can impact their ability to lead fulfilling lives and form meaningful relationships.

Moreover, the stigma and shame associated with trafficking can hinder survivors' access to support services and make it difficult for them to reintegrate into society.

Recognizing the severity and complexity of human trafficking issues is paramount for addressing this pervasive crime effectively. Urgent action is needed from law enforcement agencies and policymakers to combat the dark web and its role in facilitating illegal activities, including human trafficking. This requires enhanced collaboration and coordination among international stakeholders to dismantle trafficking networks and hold perpetrators accountable. Additionally, public awareness and education are critical for preventing human trafficking and supporting victims. By raising awareness about the tactics used by traffickers and empowering individuals to recognize and report suspicious activity, we can create a safer and more resilient society for all.

Unveiling the Reptilian Abduction Statue reveals hidden realities in plain sight. In the heart of New York City, a new statue has emerged, depicting a scene that has sparked controversy and intrigue among residents and visitors alike. This statue portrays a reptilian figure abducting a child with a bag over their head, boldly displayed in plain sight. While statues often serve as symbols of art and culture, this installation raises questions about the hidden realities lurking beneath the surface of our society. This paper delves into the significance of the reptilian abduction statue, exploring the implications of its presence and what it reveals about the concealed truths within our midst.

The unveiling of the reptilian abduction statue in New York City has not only captured the public's attention but also stirred a range of emotions, drawing both fascination and concern. The imagery of a reptilian figure abducting a child with a bag over their head is undeniably provocative, inviting speculation about its meaning and symbolism. As this statue stands prominently in a public space, its presence not only prompts us to confront uncomfortable truths but also highlights the power of art to provoke discussion and challenge societal norms.

The symbolism depicted in the reptilian abduction statue is a treasure trove of potential interpretations. Some may view it as a metaphor for the unseen forces of control and manipulation that permeate our society, represented by the reptilian figure. The abducted child, with a bag over their head, symbolizes the innocence and vulnerability of humanity while also suggesting the concealment of truth and identity. Others may interpret the statue as a commentary on conspiracy theories surrounding secret societies, extraterrestrial beings, or clandestine agendas operating in plain sight. These diverse interpretations invite us to think critically and engage in a deeper understanding of the statue's significance.

The reptilian abduction statue challenges us to confront hidden realities lurking beneath the surface of our everyday lives. It serves as a stark reminder that not everything is as it seems and that darker forces may be at play behind the scenes. By bringing these hidden truths into the light, the statue prompts us to question the narratives we are presented with and to seek a deeper understanding of the world around us.

The unveiling of the reptilian abduction statue has sparked a range of reactions from the public, ranging from curiosity to outrage. Some view it as a thought-provoking art that encourages dialogue and reflection, while others see it as a disturbing and inappropriate display in a public space. The controversy surrounding the statue highlights the power of art to provoke discussion and challenge societal norms, even when the subject matter is unsettling or controversial.

The reptilian abduction statue in New York City is a poignant reminder that hidden realities may lurk beneath our society's surface. As we grapple with its symbolism and implications, we are compelled to confront uncomfortable truths and question the narratives we are presented with. Whether viewed as a work of art, a political statement, or a disturbing revelation, the statue prompts us to seek a deeper understanding of the world around us and confront the realities hiding in plain sight.

This could happen in any of the small-town areas throughout America. Many individuals do not believe it. Many people claim it will never happen to my kid. This will never happen to our family. So, once at a time, a little girl called Em lived in this tiny town in America. Em was a brilliant and kind-hearted youngster who aspired to become a doctor and assist others.

Unfortunately, Em's life took an abrupt, dark turn when she was targeted by human traffickers, who abused her innocence and sold her into slavery. Em has suffered terrible pain and torture throughout the years, leaving her feeling helpless. However, Em hung out a glimmer of hope that she would be free and reunited with her family. Meanwhile, in the same tiny American town, a group of committed activists and volunteers worked relentlessly to stop human trafficking and assist survivors like Em. They offered refuge, therapy, and education to help other survivors reconstruct their lives and reclaim their self-esteem. One tragic day, a courageous young lady called S, a member of a volunteer organization, discovered Em in a secluded spot where she was being kept hostage. With bravery and effort, S rescued Em and took her to safety. Em gradually recovered and found her aspirations thanks to the community's persistent support and the love of her family, who never gave up hunting for her. Em got therapy, schooling, and vocational training, and with her tenacity and endurance, she finally realized her childhood ambition of becoming a physician. She serves as a light of hope and inspiration. This is a common occurrence in America. This occurs in both small and large towns. Nobody is... Nobody's... This might happen. Nobody is going... You are not immune to having this happen to your family. Human trafficking is a serious issue that parents must discuss with their children. It's a shadowy, billion-dollar business that operates on a worldwide scale. It will enter the United States. And keep in mind that American guys are the most frequent consumers of child sex.

Understanding the Complexity of Human Trafficking

Human trafficking is a multifaceted issue that intersects with various other pressing concerns, exacerbating its complexity and impact. This paper delves into the linkages between human trafficking and missing persons cases, the role of organized crime and corruption in facilitating trafficking networks, the nexus between trafficking, forced labor, and supply chains, and the impact of conflict and displacement on vulnerability to trafficking.

Human trafficking often involves the abduction or disappearance of individuals, contributing to the broader issue of missing persons. Trafficking victims may be forcibly taken from their communities or lured under pretenses, making them vulnerable to exploitation. In many cases, traffickers exploit existing vulnerabilities, such as homelessness, substance abuse, or precarious immigration status, to abduct or recruit individuals. Additionally, trafficking networks may operate in collaboration with criminal organizations involved in kidnapping or forced disappearances, further blurring the lines between trafficking and missing persons cases.

Organized crime groups play a significant role in facilitating human trafficking networks, leveraging their resources, networks, and influence to exploit vulnerable populations for profit. These criminal enterprises engage in various illicit activities, including trafficking, smuggling, and extortion, often operating across borders and in collaboration with corrupt officials. Corruption within law enforcement agencies, government institutions, and border controls enables traffickers to evade detection and prosecution, perpetuating impunity and compounding the challenges in combating trafficking effectively.

Human trafficking is intricately linked to forced labor and supply chains, particularly in industries such as agriculture, manufacturing, construction, and hospitality. Traffickers exploit vulnerable individuals, including migrants, refugees, and undocumented workers, by subjecting them to coercive labor practices, debt bondage, and exploitation. These forced laborers often produce goods and services that end up in global supply chains, perpetuating a cycle of exploitation and complicity. Addressing trafficking in supply chains requires robust oversight, transparency, and accountability measures to ensure ethical labor practices and prevent the exploitation of workers.

Conflict and displacement significantly increase vulnerability to trafficking, exposing populations to exploitation, abuse, and forced displacement. Displaced persons, including refugees, asylum seekers, and internally displaced individuals, are at heightened risk of trafficking due to their precarious circumstances, lack of legal protections, and limited access to resources. Conflict zones create environments conducive to trafficking, with armed groups and criminal networks preying on vulnerable populations for recruitment, exploitation, and ransom. Addressing the root causes of conflict, promoting peacebuilding initiatives, and providing support and protection to displaced persons are essential for mitigating vulnerability to trafficking in conflict-affected regions. Understanding the intersection between human trafficking and other issues is vital to developing comprehensive strategies to combat trafficking effectively. By addressing the linkages between trafficking and missing persons cases, organized crime and corruption, forced labor and supply chains, and conflict and displacement, stakeholders can work towards holistic solutions that protect the rights and dignity of all individuals and create a more just and equitable society.

Raising Awareness and Taking Action: Mobilizing Efforts Against Human Trafficking. In the fight against human trafficking, raising awareness and taking action are paramount. This paper explores various avenues for mobilizing efforts, including media representation and storytelling, grassroots activism, corporate social responsibility, and individual actions within communities.

Media, including documentaries, films, literature, and news coverage, shapes public perceptions and understanding of human trafficking. Documentaries such as "Nefarious: Merchant of Souls" and movies like "Taken" have shed light on the horrors of trafficking, exposing audiences to the realities faced by victims and survivors. Literature, including memoirs and investigative journalism, provides nuanced insights into the complexities of trafficking and its impact on individuals and communities. By amplifying survivor voices, challenging stereotypes, and exposing the root causes of trafficking, media representation, and storytelling can foster empathy, raise awareness, and inspire action.

Grassroots activism and advocacy efforts are crucial in mobilizing communities and driving systemic change. Non-profit organizations, community groups, and grassroots movements work tirelessly to raise awareness, provide support services to survivors, and advocate for policy reform. Grassroots activists organize rallies, marches, and awareness campaigns to educate the public about trafficking and pressure governments to take action. Grassroots activism catalyzes social change and justice by empowering survivors, amplifying their voices, and mobilizing community support.

Corporate social responsibility (CSR) and ethical consumption are vital to combating human trafficking. Companies and businesses are responsible for ensuring that their supply chains are free from exploitation and forced labor. By implementing ethical sourcing policies, conducting supply chain audits, and collaborating with stakeholders, companies can mitigate the risk of trafficking and promote fair labor practices. Consumers also play a pivotal role in driving demand for ethical products and holding companies accountable for their actions. By making informed purchasing decisions and supporting businesses that prioritize ethical practices, consumers can leverage their purchasing power to combat trafficking and promote social responsibility.

Individual actions and community involvement are instrumental in combating human trafficking at the grassroots level. By educating themselves about the signs of trafficking, individuals can recognize and report suspicious activities to authorities. Community members can also support local organizations and initiatives working to prevent trafficking, support survivors, and raise awareness in their communities. From hosting educational events to volunteering at shelters, every individual has the power to make a difference in the fight against trafficking. By fostering a culture of vigilance, empathy, and collective action, communities can create safer environments and protect the most vulnerable from exploitation. Raising awareness and taking action are essential components of combating human trafficking. Through media representation and storytelling, grassroots activism, corporate social responsibility, and individual actions within communities, stakeholders can mobilize efforts, challenge systemic injustices, and create a world where every individual is free from exploitation and oppression.

Indeed, the vision of a future where human trafficking is eradicated and the voices of survivors are heard and respected is both hopeful and achievable. This future requires concerted efforts from individuals, communities, governments, and organizations worldwide to address the root causes of trafficking, support survivors, and uphold human rights.

To realize this vision, it is crucial to prioritize prevention through education, awareness campaigns, and economic empowerment initiatives. By addressing factors such as poverty, inequality, lack of education, and social marginalization, we can mitigate vulnerabilities to trafficking and empower individuals to make informed choices about their lives.

Additionally, robust legal frameworks and effective law enforcement mechanisms are essential for holding traffickers accountable and ensuring justice for survivors. This includes strengthening anti-trafficking legislation, enhancing collaboration between law enforcement agencies, and providing adequate resources for victim support and rehabilitation services.

Fostering a culture of empathy, compassion, and solidarity is vital for creating supportive environments where survivors feel empowered to speak out and seek assistance without fear of stigma or reprisal. Their voices are not just important, they are the guiding light in our fight against trafficking. Centering survivor voices in anti-trafficking efforts ensures that policies and interventions are informed by their experiences and needs, making our efforts more effective and meaningful.

Corporate responsibility is not just a buzzword; it's a significant tool for eradicating trafficking. Businesses can play a pivotal role in this fight by ensuring ethical labor practices and supply chain transparency. By holding businesses accountable for their actions and supporting ethical consumption, consumers can drive demand for fair and sustainable practices. This is not just a call to action; it's a responsibility we all share.

Ultimately, eradicating human trafficking requires a comprehensive and collaborative approach that addresses the root causes, supports survivors, and promotes a culture of human dignity and respect. By working together towards this common goal, we can build a future where exploitation and injustice have no place, and everyone can live free from fear and exploitation.

Bridging the Divide and Understanding the Nuances of Sex and Labor Trafficking Investigations When delving into the complexities of human trafficking investigations, it becomes apparent that sex and labor trafficking present distinct challenges and nuances. Examining data from federally funded human trafficking task forces sheds light on significant differences between the two forms of exploitation, urging us to critically assess the strategies employed in combating these egregious crimes.

Firstly, analysis reveals that 25% of sex trafficking cases involve multiple victims, whereas over 50% of labor trafficking cases do. Moreover, sex trafficking victims tend to be younger than their labor trafficking counterparts, with one-third fewer victims under the age of 18. Local law enforcement agencies predominantly lead investigations into sex trafficking cases, accounting for 85% of all trafficking cases compared to 60% of labor trafficking cases.

However, despite these statistics, the efficacy of investigations and prosecutions remains a pressing concern. Less than half of the sex trafficking cases investigated by local law enforcement result in arrest, and over half of the arrests do not lead to prosecution. This alarming trend underscores the urgent need for improved strategies and resources to enhance the investigative and prosecutorial processes.

Over the years, efforts to combat human trafficking have been bolstered by legislative reforms in 43 states, criminalizing these heinous acts and facilitating prosecution. Notably, Alabama recently enacted the Sound of Freedom Act (House Bill 42), imposing mandatory life sentences for trafficking minors and survivors who are minors. This landmark legislation signifies a pivotal step towards eradicating juvenile human trafficking and holding perpetrators accountable for their crimes.

Yet, challenges persist, particularly in data collection and analysis. The lack of comprehensive data undermines our ability to accurately assess the scope of the problem and develop targeted interventions. Collaborative efforts between nonprofits and law enforcement agencies are essential in bridging this gap, facilitating the collection and dissemination of vital information to communities, schools, and households.

Ultimately, addressing human trafficking requires a concerted, multifaceted approach that transcends traditional boundaries. By harnessing the power of data, fostering collaboration between stakeholders, and empowering communities with knowledge and resources, we can combat human trafficking at its roots and safeguard the most vulnerable among us. Together, we can build a future where exploitation and victimization are relics of the past, and every individual can live free from fear and coercion.

Understanding the Link between Missing Persons Cases and Human Trafficking

The intersection between missing person cases and human trafficking unveils the intricate and interconnected nature of these crimes. Within this intersection lies a web of systemic issues that exacerbate vulnerabilities and impede effective responses to these grave injustices.

Many missing person cases involve individuals who have been abducted, coerced, or deceived into trafficking situations. Traffickers exploit vulnerable individuals, such as runaways, homeless youth, or migrants, leveraging their precarious situations for profit. In some instances, missing persons may be trafficked for various forms of exploitation, including forced labor, sexual exploitation, or organ trafficking. Recognizing this link between missing persons cases and trafficking is pivotal for identifying and responding to victims, as well as for preventing further victimization.

Furthermore, broader systemic issues contribute to both missing persons cases and human trafficking. These encompass socioeconomic inequalities, limited access to education and economic opportunities, systemic racism and discrimination, inadequate social support systems, and gaps in child welfare and protection services. Marginalized and disadvantaged populations are disproportionately affected by these systemic issues, heightening their vulnerability to exploitation and victimization.

Additionally, systemic failures within law enforcement, legal systems, and social services perpetuate the cycle of impunity for traffickers and impede efforts to support and protect victims. Insufficient resources, training, and coordination among agencies often result in inadequate responses to missing persons cases and trafficking investigations. Moreover, corruption and complicity among officials may enable traffickers to operate with impunity, further undermining efforts to combat these crimes.

Addressing the intersectionality between missing person cases and human trafficking necessitates a multifaceted approach that tackles root causes, enhances prevention efforts, strengthens victim support services, and improves collaboration among stakeholders. This entails investing in education and economic opportunities for marginalized communities, fortifying child welfare and protection systems, bolstering law enforcement capabilities and training, and advocating for survivor-centered approaches to support and rehabilitation. By addressing the broader systemic issues that perpetuate these crimes, we can create a safer and more equitable society where exploitation and trafficking are less likely to occur.

Advocating for a comprehensive approach to addressing missing persons and human trafficking is paramount for combating these grave injustices and safeguarding vulnerable individuals. Transparency, accountability, and scrutiny of those in positions of power are critical components of such an approach. Exposing and dismantling clandestine networks involved in human trafficking requires concerted efforts to uncover and hold accountable those responsible for perpetuating these crimes, including individuals within elite circles who exploit their wealth, influence, and connections to evade scrutiny and manipulate the justice system. By increasing transparency and accountability within institutions, we can create an environment where perpetrators are less able to operate with impunity.

Shedding light on the intersectionality between missing person cases and human trafficking is crucial. Many individuals who go missing may become trapped in trafficking networks, making it imperative to address both issues concurrently. Collaborative efforts between law enforcement agencies, non-governmental organizations, and other stakeholders are essential to effectively identify, rescue, and support victims while holding perpetrators accountable.

In advocating for increased transparency, accountability, and scrutiny of those in positions of power, we emphasize the importance of empowering survivors, amplifying their voices, and ensuring that their experiences are heard and respected. By working together to expose and dismantle these networks, we can create a safer and more just world where human rights are upheld, and justice is served for all victims of trafficking and exploitation.

Identifying Organized Community Pedophile Ring Recognition & Reaction Mechanisms

Pedophile rings represent a dark underbelly of organized communities, where vulnerable individuals, particularly children, become victims of heinous crimes. The intricate workings of the pedophile ring, exploring their tactics, recruitment methods, and the psychological manipulation employed to perpetrate abuse. By providing insights into how these rings operate and offering guidance on recognizing their presence, this paper aims to empower communities to identify and combat this pervasive threat.

Pedophile rings operate as clandestine networks within organized communities, preying on the innocence of children and exploiting their vulnerabilities for the gratification of perpetrators. Understanding the mechanisms by which these rings function is crucial for recognizing their existence and taking decisive action to protect potential victims.

Pedophile rings employ sophisticated grooming techniques to recruit vulnerable children into their fold, perpetuating a cycle of exploitation and abuse. This paper aims to shed light on the recruitment tactics utilized by pedophile rings, with a focus on online platforms and social media. Drawing on research, case studies, and expert insights, the paper examines how perpetrators exploit positions of trust, utilize online anonymity, and manipulate victims to gain their trust. Furthermore, it proposes strategies for prevention, intervention, and law enforcement collaboration to combat online exploitation and protect children from falling prey to pedophile rings.

Pedophile rings represent a sinister underworld where vulnerable children are targeted and exploited for the gratification of perpetrators. This section introduces the prevalence of online exploitation by pedophile rings and underscores the critical need for comprehensive responses to combat this pervasive threat.

Pedophile rings operate within a shadowy realm, utilizing grooming techniques as a cornerstone of their predatory behavior. This paper aims to dissect the intricate methods employed by these rings to trap and victimize individuals, particularly children. By unraveling the process of grooming, we can better understand how perpetrators exploit trust, manipulate emotions, and normalize abusive behavior, ultimately empowering communities to recognize and combat these insidious tactics.

Grooming often begins with perpetrators strategically cultivating trust and rapport with their intended victims. Leveraging positions of authority, feigned benevolence, or targeted grooming tactics, perpetrators gradually ingratiate themselves into the lives of vulnerable individuals. By portraying themselves as trustworthy and dependable figures, they create a facade of safety and security that lulls victims into a false sense of security.

Once trust is established, perpetrators employ a myriad of emotional manipulation techniques to solidify their control over victims. They may shower victims with attention, affection, and validation, exploiting their emotional vulnerabilities and fostering a sense of dependence. Through gaslighting, subtle coercion, and psychological conditioning, perpetrators erode victims' self-esteem and agency, paving the way for further exploitation.

As the grooming process progresses, perpetrators systematically desensitize victims to increasingly inappropriate and boundary-violating behavior. By gradually introducing sexual or exploitative acts under the guise of affection or special treatment, they normalize and justify their actions while instilling feelings of confusion, shame, and powerlessness in their victims. This gradual erosion of boundaries and moral compasses makes it increasingly difficult for victims to recognize the abuse and seek help.

The psychological repercussions of grooming are profound and enduring, leaving victims traumatized and emotionally scarred. Victims often grapple with feelings of guilt, shame, and self-blame, compounded by the emotional bonds forged during the grooming process. These complex emotions can impede victims' ability to disclose the abuse, seek assistance, or break free from the perpetrator's influence, perpetuating the cycle of victimization and silence.

To illustrate the devastating consequences of grooming, this paper provides case studies and real-world examples of pedophile rings in action. These narratives underscore the calculated nature of grooming tactics, as well as the profound impact on victims and their families. By highlighting the lived experiences of survivors, we gain insight into the manipulative strategies employed by perpetrators and the urgent need for prevention and intervention measures.

Grooming techniques wielded by pedophile rings represent a grave threat to the safety and well-being of vulnerable individuals. By dissecting these insidious tactics, we can arm ourselves with the knowledge and awareness needed to identify grooming behavior, support victims, and disrupt the cycle of abuse. It is imperative that we remain vigilant, proactive, and united in our efforts to dismantle pedophile rings and protect the most vulnerable members of our communities from exploitation and harm.

Pedophile rings often exploit positions of trust, such as authority figures, mentors, and community leaders, to gain access to potential victims. This section examines how perpetrators leverage their perceived authority and influence to groom victims and establish relationships based on deceit and manipulation.

With the advent of digital technology, pedophile rings increasingly utilize online platforms and social media to recruit and groom victims. This section analyzes how perpetrators exploit the anonymity afforded by the Internet to conceal their identities and prey on vulnerable children in virtual spaces.

Perpetrators employ a range of manipulative tactics to deceive and coerce victims into engaging in inappropriate behavior. This section explores the tactics used by pedophile rings, including threats, promises, and emotional manipulation, to exert control over their victims.

Proactive prevention and intervention strategies are essential to combat online exploitation. This section proposes a multifaceted approach, including education and awareness campaigns, online safety training for children and caregivers, and establishing reporting mechanisms to facilitate early intervention.

Collaboration among law enforcement agencies, technology companies, and advocacy groups is crucial in combating online exploitation. This section emphasizes the importance of coordinated efforts to dismantle pedophile rings, hold perpetrators accountable, and protect vulnerable children from harm.

There is an urgent need to address the recruitment tactics of pedophile rings operating in online spaces. By understanding the methods employed by perpetrators and implementing proactive measures for prevention and intervention, stakeholders can work together to safeguard children from exploitation and abuse in the digital age.

Understanding and Combating Online Exploitation of Pedophile Rings utilize covert communication channels to orchestrate their illegal activities while evading detection by law enforcement and community members. This paper delves into the intricate web of covert communication tactics employed by pedophile rings, with a focus on encryption tools, secret codes, and encrypted messaging apps. Drawing insights from research findings, case studies, and expert analysis, the paper explores how these clandestine communication methods facilitate coordination among perpetrators, enabling them to perpetrate abuse, share illicit content, and circumvent authorities. Furthermore, the paper presents strategies for law enforcement agencies, technology providers, and communities to counteract covert communication and disrupt the operations of pedophile rings.

Pedophile rings represent a sinister underworld where covert communication plays a pivotal role in orchestrating heinous crimes against children. In this shadowy realm, perpetrators exploit advanced technology and psychological manipulation tactics to evade detection and maintain control over their victims. This section aims to introduce the prevalence and significance of covert communication tactics within pedophile rings, setting the stage for a comprehensive exploration of these insidious practices.

The use of covert communication channels by pedophile rings has escalated with the proliferation of digital technology and online platforms. These clandestine networks operate in the shadows of the Internet, exploiting encryption tools, secret codes, and encrypted messaging apps to facilitate communication and coordination among members. By leveraging sophisticated technology, perpetrators can evade detection by law enforcement and community members, creating an environment of impunity where they can carry out their nefarious activities.

Moreover, psychological manipulation tactics are wielded with precision by pedophile rings to control and exploit their victims. Through gaslighting, grooming, and emotional coercion, perpetrators instill fear, shame, and secrecy in their victims, effectively silencing them and preventing disclosure of abuse. Victims, often vulnerable and impressionable, find themselves entangled in a web of deceit and manipulation, unable to break free from the grip of their abusers.

Understanding the prevalence and significance of covert communication tactics within pedophile rings is crucial for effective prevention and intervention efforts. By shedding light on these dark practices, stakeholders can develop targeted strategies to detect, disrupt, and dismantle pedophile networks, ultimately safeguarding children from exploitation and abuse. We can strive to eradicate this scourge and create a safer world for all through collaboration, vigilance, and a commitment to justice.

Pedophile rings operate within a clandestine network where communication is shrouded in secrecy to evade detection and accountability. This section aims to elucidate the mechanics of covert communication channels utilized by pedophile rings, with a focus on encryption tools, secret codes, and encrypted messaging apps.

Encryption tools serve as a cornerstone of covert communication within pedophile rings. These tools utilize advanced algorithms to encode messages, rendering them unreadable to anyone without the corresponding decryption key. By encrypting their communications, perpetrators can communicate securely without fear of interception or surveillance by law enforcement authorities. Encryption tools range from simple software applications to sophisticated encryption protocols, providing pedophile rings with a secure means of communication across various digital platforms.

In addition to encryption tools, pedophile rings often employ secret codes to conceal the true nature of their communications. These codes may involve substituting words or phrases with coded language or using symbols and gestures to convey hidden messages. By using secret codes, perpetrators can communicate covertly while minimizing the risk of detection by external parties. Secret codes may be shared among members of the pedophile ring through trusted channels or established protocols, further enhancing the clandestine nature of their communication.

Encrypted messaging apps have emerged as a preferred communication tool for pedophile rings due to their robust security features and anonymity. These apps utilize end-to-end encryption, ensuring that only the sender and intended recipient can decipher the contents of a message. Additionally, many encrypted messaging apps offer features such as self-destructing messages and anonymous registration, further enhancing the privacy and security of communications. By leveraging encrypted messaging apps, pedophile rings can coordinate their activities with impunity, shielded from scrutiny by law enforcement and other stakeholders.

Covert communication channels play a crucial role in facilitating criminal activities within pedophile rings. By enabling secure and discreet communication, encryption tools, secret codes, and encrypted messaging apps empower perpetrators to coordinate abuse, share illicit content, and evade detection by authorities. These clandestine communication methods create a veil of secrecy around the activities of pedophile rings, making it challenging for law enforcement agencies to identify and disrupt their operations.

Moreover, covert communication channels contribute to the normalization and perpetuation of abusive behaviors within pedophile rings. By providing a platform for perpetrators to communicate and collaborate, these channels reinforce group dynamics and solidarity among members, reinforcing their sense of impunity and invincibility. As a result, victims may find themselves isolated and powerless, further entrenching the cycle of exploitation and abuse.

Understanding the mechanics of covert communication channels utilized by pedophile rings is essential for effective prevention and intervention efforts. By shining a light on these clandestine practices, stakeholders can develop targeted strategies to disrupt pedophile networks, safeguard vulnerable children, and hold perpetrators accountable for their actions. Through collaboration, innovation, and a commitment to justice, we can strive to dismantle pedophile rings and create a safer world for all.

Pedophile rings leverage encryption tools and techniques to safeguard their communication channels and identities from law enforcement scrutiny. This section provides an in-depth analysis of the encryption methods these criminal networks favor.

Encryption serves as a cornerstone of covert communication within pedophile rings, allowing perpetrators to exchange sensitive information securely and without fear of interception. Advanced encryption algorithms scramble the contents of messages, making them unreadable to anyone without the decryption key. This ensures that communications remain confidential and inaccessible to external parties, including law enforcement agencies.

Pedophile rings utilize various encryption tools and techniques to secure their communication channels. End-to-end encryption encrypts messages so only the sender and intended recipient can decipher the contents. This ensures that even the service provider facilitating the communication cannot access the plaintext. Pedophile rings often rely on messaging apps and platforms that offer end-to-end encryption to safeguard the confidentiality of their communications. Encryption protocols, such as SSL/TLS (Secure Sockets Layer/Transport Layer Security), are commonly used to secure communication over the Internet. These protocols encrypt data transmitted between devices, preventing eavesdroppers from intercepting and deciphering the information. Pedophile rings may employ encryption protocols to protect their online activities, including file sharing and data exchange. VPNs create a secure and encrypted connection between a user's device and a remote server, masking the user's IP address and encrypting their internet traffic. By routing their communication through VPNs, perpetrators can obscure their online activities and evade detection by law enforcement authorities.

In addition to encryption, pedophile rings utilize secret codes and symbols as covert communication mechanisms to conceal illicit activities and coordinate their operations. This section explores how these clandestine signals are employed within pedophile networks.

Secret codes and symbols allow perpetrators to communicate discreetly while minimizing the risk of detection by external parties. These codes may involve substituting words or phrases with coded language, using symbols and gestures to convey hidden messages, or employing specific terminology understood only by members of the pedophile ring.

Examples of secret codes and symbols used by pedophiles may use codewords or phrases to refer to illicit activities or individuals involved in their network. These codewords are often innocuous-sounding terms with a hidden meaning understood only by group members. Pedophile rings may use symbols, icons, or logos to identify themselves or signal their involvement in illicit activities. These symbols may be shared discreetly in online forums, social media profiles, or physical locations frequented by group members. In some cases, pedophiles may use hand signals or gestures to communicate covertly in person or during online interactions. These signals may be used to convey messages or indicate membership in the pedophile ring without attracting attention from outsiders. Overall, secret codes and symbols play a crucial role in facilitating covert communication within pedophile rings, allowing perpetrators to coordinate their activities and evade detection by law enforcement authorities. Understanding these communication mechanisms is essential for developing effective strategies to combat online exploitation and protect vulnerable children from harm.

Pedophile rings exploit encrypted messaging apps as a sanctuary for their covert communication endeavors, shielding their activities from the scrutiny of authorities and community members. This section delves into the characteristics and implications of encrypted messaging platforms in the context of online exploitation.

Encrypted messaging apps, such as WhatsApp, Signal, and Telegram, offer pedophile rings a secure and private environment to communicate, collaborate, and exchange illicit content without fear of interception or surveillance. These platforms employ end-to-end encryption, ensuring that only the sender and recipient can access the contents of messages, effectively rendering them indecipherable to third parties, including law enforcement agencies.

The anonymity afforded by encrypted messaging apps further facilitates clandestine communication among pedophile networks. Perpetrators can create pseudonymous accounts without revealing their true identities, making it challenging for authorities to trace their activities or identify individuals involved in illicit behavior.

Moreover, encrypted messaging apps provide pedophile rings with features tailored to their nefarious purposes. These platforms often include functionalities such as self-destructing messages, where conversations automatically delete after a specified period, minimizing the risk of discovering incriminating evidence.

The practical application of covert communication tactics within pedophile rings is exemplified through case studies and real-world examples, shedding light on the profound impact of such tactics on victims and the formidable challenges faced by law enforcement agencies.

Operation Endeavor uncovered a pedophile ring operating on encrypted messaging apps, orchestrating the distribution of child sexual abuse material (CSAM), and facilitating online grooming and exploitation of minors. Perpetrators utilized end-to-end encryption to shield their conversations from detection, complicating efforts by law enforcement to identify and apprehend individuals involved in the network. Through extensive investigative efforts and collaboration with international partners, authorities successfully dismantled the ring, resulting in the arrest and prosecution of multiple perpetrators and the rescue of numerous victims.

In a disturbing case they were reported globally, a perpetrator utilized WhatsApp, an encrypted messaging app, to groom and exploit underage victims. The perpetrator masqueraded as a trustworthy figure, gaining the trust of vulnerable children and coercing them into engaging in sexually explicit conversations and activities. Despite suspicions raised by concerned parents and community members, the encrypted nature of WhatsApp communications impeded efforts to intervene and hold the perpetrator accountable. The case underscores the challenges posed by encrypted messaging apps in combating online exploitation and protecting children from harm.

These case studies and examples underscore the critical importance of addressing covert communication tactics within pedophile rings and highlight the urgent need for collaborative efforts to combat online exploitation, safeguard vulnerable children, and hold perpetrators accountable for their crimes.

Law enforcement agencies confront significant hurdles in their efforts to combat the covert communication tactics employed by pedophile rings. This section elucidates the formidable challenges authorities encounter, ranging from technological limitations to jurisdictional complexities and resource constraints.

Law enforcement agencies grapple with technological limitations that impede their ability to effectively monitor and intercept covert communication channels utilized by pedophile rings. Encryption technologies, such as end-to-end encryption employed by messaging apps, pose a significant barrier, rendering communications indecipherable to third parties, including law enforcement. As a result, authorities face challenges accessing crucial evidence and gathering intelligence to investigate and prosecute perpetrators.

The transnational nature of online exploitation presents jurisdictional complexities for law enforcement agencies, exacerbating the challenges of combating pedophile rings. Perpetrators operate across international borders, leveraging the anonymity and reach of the Internet to evade legal consequences. Coordination and cooperation among law enforcement agencies across jurisdictions are essential to address these challenges effectively. However, disparities in legal frameworks, jurisdictional boundaries, and diplomatic considerations often hinder seamless collaboration and impede efforts to disrupt pedophile networks.

Law enforcement agencies confront resource constraints that limit their capacity to investigate and combat covert communication tactics utilized by pedophile rings. Budgetary constraints, staffing shortages, and competing priorities divert attention and resources from efforts to address online exploitation effectively. Additionally, the rapid evolution of technology necessitates ongoing investment in specialized training, equipment, and infrastructure to keep pace with perpetrators' tactics and techniques.

Despite the formidable challenges faced by law enforcement, this section proposes a range of strategies for detecting and disrupting covert communication channels within pedophile rings.

Law enforcement agencies can leverage advanced surveillance techniques and technological tools to monitor online activities and identify suspicious behavior indicative of pedophile networks. This may involve deploying specialized software, data analytics, and digital forensics capabilities to track and trace communication patterns and identify individuals involved in online exploitation.

Collaboration between law enforcement agencies and technology providers is essential for combating covert communication tactics employed by pedophile rings. By engaging with technology companies, authorities can advocate for measures to enhance platform security, facilitate lawful access to encrypted communications under appropriate legal frameworks, and develop tools and protocols for detecting and reporting illicit activity.

Initiatives for community participation are essential for identifying and closing secret lines of communication inside pedophile networks. Empowering individuals and communities to recognize the signs of online exploitation, report suspicious behavior, and access support services is essential for enhancing vigilance and resilience against pedophile networks. Law enforcement agencies can collaborate with community organizations, schools, and online safety advocates to raise awareness, provide education and training, and foster a culture of accountability and responsibility in safeguarding children from online harm.

Fighting pedophile networks requires a delicate balance between privacy rights and ethical issues. While safeguarding children from exploitation is paramount, it is essential to uphold fundamental rights and liberties, including privacy and due process. Law enforcement agencies must adhere to legal and ethical standards in their investigative practices, ensuring that interventions are proportionate, justified, and respectful of individuals' rights. Maintaining public confidence in law enforcement's efforts to prevent internet exploitation requires transparency, accountability, and monitoring systems.

Addressing the challenges posed by covert communication tactics within pedophile rings requires a multifaceted approach involving technological innovation, collaboration, and ethical considerations. By leveraging advanced surveillance techniques, enhancing cooperation with technology providers, engaging communities, and upholding ethical standards, law enforcement agencies can improve their capacity to detect and disrupt pedophile networks effectively while safeguarding individual rights and liberties. Collaboration among stakeholders, including government agencies, technology companies, civil society organizations, and communities, is essential for developing comprehensive strategies to combat online exploitation and protect children from harm.

Covert Communication and Psychological Manipulation

Pedophile rings employ covert communication channels and psychological manipulation tactics to evade detection and control their victims. This paper aims to explore the insidious methods used by pedophile rings, including encryption tools, secret codes, and psychological manipulation techniques. Drawing on research, case studies, and expert insights, the paper examines how perpetrators exploit technology to facilitate communication while manipulating victims to maintain secrecy and control. Furthermore, it proposes strategies for law enforcement and community members to detect and combat these tactics, ultimately protecting vulnerable individuals from exploitation and abuse.

Pedophile rings represent a clandestine network where perpetrators exploit covert communication channels and psychological manipulation tactics to control their victims and evade detection. This section introduces the prevalence of pedophile rings and the critical need to understand their tactics for effective prevention and intervention.

Pedophile rings rely on covert communication channels to evade detection by law enforcement and community members. This section explores how perpetrators utilize encryption tools, secret codes, and encrypted messaging apps to facilitate communication and coordination among members. By operating in the shadows of the Internet, perpetrators can coordinate abuse and share illicit content while remaining undetected by authorities.

Perpetrators employ a range of psychological manipulation tactics to control and manipulate their victims. This section delves into how perpetrators use gaslighting, grooming, and emotional coercion to instill fear, shame, and secrecy in their victims. By exploiting vulnerabilities such as low self-esteem or familial discord, perpetrators can exert influence and maintain control over their victims, preventing disclosure of abuse.

The psychological manipulation tactics employed by pedophile rings have a devastating impact on victims, leading to long-term trauma and psychological harm. This section examines the emotional and psychological consequences experienced by victims, including feelings of isolation, guilt, and self-blame. By understanding the impact of psychological manipulation, stakeholders can better support victims and provide effective interventions.

Detecting and combating the tactics of pedophile rings requires a multidimensional approach involving law enforcement, technology companies, and community members. This section proposes strategies for identifying covert communication channels and recognizing signs of psychological manipulation. By raising awareness, enhancing digital literacy, and promoting reporting mechanisms, stakeholders can work together to disrupt pedophile rings and protect vulnerable individuals from exploitation.

Behavioral Indicators Pedophile rings operate covertly, making it crucial for individuals and communities to be vigilant and aware of behavioral indicators that may signal the presence of exploitation. This section outlines vital behavioral indicators that may suggest the involvement of pedophile rings, focusing on changes in behavior, online activities, and interactions with adults or older peers.

One of the most significant red flags indicating potential grooming or abuse by pedophile rings is unexplained changes in a child's behavior, mood, or academic performance. These changes may manifest as sudden withdrawal, anxiety, depression, or a decline in educational achievement. Children who are being groomed or abused may exhibit signs of distress, including nightmares, bedwetting, or self-harm. Paying attention to such behavioral shifts and addressing them promptly can help identify and intervene in exploitation cases.

Pedophile rings often utilize online platforms and social media to groom and exploit victims, making secretive behavior regarding online activities a concerning indicator. Children who are involved with pedophile rings may exhibit secrecy regarding their internet usage, such as hiding screens or devices, avoiding discussions about online interactions, or becoming defensive when questioned about their online activities. Parents and caregivers should establish open communication with children about internet safety and encourage them to report any concerning online encounters.

Children who are being groomed or abused by pedophile rings may exhibit reluctance or discomfort in discussing interactions with specific individuals, mainly adults or older peers involved in the exploitation. Perpetrators often manipulate victims into maintaining secrecy by instilling fear, shame, or confusion. Parents, educators, and caregivers should be attentive to signs of discomfort or avoidance when discussing relationships with specific individuals and create a safe space for children to express concerns without fear of judgment or reprisal.

Perpetrators within pedophile rings often employ grooming tactics that involve offering sudden gifts, favors, or special attention to their intended victims. Children who are targeted by pedophile rings may receive lavish gifts, preferential treatment, or undue attention from adults or older peers, creating a sense of indebtedness or obligation. Parents and caregivers should be wary of such behavior and investigate the motives behind excessive gifts or attention, particularly when they come from individuals outside the child's immediate family or trusted circle of friends.

It is crucial to identify the behavioral cues linked to pedophile rings to protect kids from abuse and exploitation. Through vig lance and attentiveness towards behavioral, psychological, online, and interpersonal changes, people and communities may detect possible indicators of child exploitation or grooming and take proactive measures to safeguard vulnerable children. To stop pedophile rings from spreading and to create safe spaces where kids can grow, it's essential to have open lines of communication, educate people about internet safety, and build trustworthy connections.

Recognizing Suspicious Activities Linked to Pedophile Rings Pedophile rings often operate under the radar, engaging in secretive behaviors and activities to conceal their exploitation of children. Understanding and recognizing suspicious activities associated with pedophile networks is crucial for protecting vulnerable individuals and communities. This section outlines critical indicators of suspicious activities that may signal the presence of pedophile rings, emphasizing the importance of vigilance and reporting concerns to authorities.

One of the hallmark signs of pedophile rings is the organization of unusual or secretive gatherings involving children and adults, particularly in isolated or private settings. These gatherings may take place under the guise of legitimate activities, such as social events, clubs, or mentoring programs, but serve as opportunities for perpetrators to groom and exploit vulnerable children. Adults who organize or participate in such gatherings may exhibit manipulative behavior, exerting influence over children and isolating them from their families or trusted support networks. Community members should be vigilant and report any suspicious gatherings involving children and adults to local authorities for further investigation.

Pedophile rings frequently utilize online platforms and social media to groom and exploit victims, making suspicious online behavior a significant indicator of potential involvement in such networks. Individuals involved d in pedophile rings may engage in secretive online interactions, frequent visits to inappropriate websites, or the exchange of illicit content. Children who are targeted by pedophile rings may also exhibit secretive behavior online, such as hiding screens or devices, using encrypted messaging apps, or receiving unsolicited requests or invitations from unknown individuals. Parents, educators, and caregivers should monitor children's online activities closely and report any concerning behavior to appropriate authorities or online safety organizations for intervention.

Reports or rumors of individuals offering opportunities for children to engage in secretive or illicit activities should be taken seriously and reported to authorities promptly. Perpetrators with pedophile rings may use promises of special privileges, rewards, or experiences to lure children into exploitative situations, exploiting their vulnerabilities and naivety. Community members ho become aware of suspicious offers or invitations targeting children should report their concerns to law enforcement agencies, child protection services, or trusted advocacy organizations specializing in the prevention of child exploitation and abuse.

Recognizing and responding to suspicious activities linked to pedophile rings is essential for safeguarding children and communities from exploitation and abuse. By remaining vigilant and proactive in reporting concerns to authorities, individuals can play a crucial role in disrupting pedophile networks and ensuring the safety and well-being of vulnerable children. Education, awareness, and community engagement are vital to practical prevention efforts, fostering environments where children are protected, supported, and empowered to thrive.

Pedophile rings represent a grave threat to the safety and well-being of children within organized communities. By understanding the mechanics of these rings and recognizing the warning signs of their presence, communities can take proactive steps to protect potential victims and hold perpetrators accountable. Through vigilance, education, and collaborative efforts, we can work towards creating safer environments for all individuals, free from the scourge of pedophile networks.

Trusting Instincts and Empowering Prevention: Recognizing the Presence of Pedophile Rings

Trusting instincts and maintaining vigilance regarding potential signs of abuse or exploitation are paramount in identifying the presence of pedophile rings within communities. By acknowledging the significance of gut feelings and subtle cues, individuals can play a vital role in safeguarding vulnerable individuals, particularly children, from falling victim to exploitation. This section under-cores the importance of trusting instincts, fostering open communication with children, and educating oneself and others about the tactics and warning signs of pedophile rings as crucial components of prevention efforts.

Trusting one's instincts and intuition is often the first line of defense in recognizing the presence of pedophile rings and protecting potential victims. Intuitive feelings of discomfort, suspicion, or unease in certain situations or interactions may serve as red flags, signaling potential risks of abuse or exploitation. Individuals should acknowledge and trust these instincts, understanding that they may pick up on subtle cues or behaviors that warrant further investigation or intervention. Individuals can take proactive steps to prevent harm and promote safety within their communities by validating and acting upon these instincts.

Fostering open communication with children and creating a safe environment for disclosure is essential in empowering victims to come forward and seek help when faced with abuse or exploitation. Children should feel comfortable expressing their thoughts, feelings, and concerns without fear of judgment or reprisal. Adults, including arents, caregivers, educators, and community members, should actively listen to children, validate their experiences, and offer support and assistance when needed. By promoting trust and transparency in relationships with children, adults can facilitate early detection and intervention in cases of potential abuse or exploitation linked to pedophile rings.

Possible Pedophile Ring Links in Shannon Paulk Cold Case

The disappearance and murder of Shannon Paulk, an 11-year-old girl from Prattville, Alabama, in 2001 sent shockwaves through the local community and left investigators grasping for answers. Despite extensive efforts to solve the case, Shannon's killer remains at large, and the truth behind her death remains elusive. However, as we delve deeper into the details of Shannon Paulk's cold case, we begin to uncover disturbing evidence suggesting possible ties to a pedophile ring operating in the area.

Shannon's case is not merely a tragic story of a young girl's untimely demise; it is also a stark reminder of the pervasive threat of child exploitation and the sinister activities of pedophile networks. As we examine the evidence, draw on investigative findings and insights, and our own research, a disturbing pattern begins to emerge. There are indications that Shannon's abduction and murder may not have been isolated incidents but rather part of a larger scheme orchestrated by those preying on vulnerable children.

The modus operandi of pedophile rings often involves the systematic grooming of victims, manipulation of trust, and exploitation of vulnerabilities. In Shannon's case, some elements suggest she may have been targeted by individuals with connections to such a network. The circumstances surrounding her disappearance, the lack of conclusive evidence pointing to a single perpetrator, and the presence of suspicious activities in the community all point to the possibility of a larger conspiracy at play.

As we piece together the puzzle of Shannon Paulk's cold case, it becomes increasingly apparent that unraveling the truth requires a closer examination of the shadowy world of pedophile rings. By shedding light on this overlooked aspect of the case, we hope to contribute to ongoing efforts to bring justice for Shannon and other victims of child exploitation. Our investigation is not only about solving a decades-old mystery but also about exposing the dark underbelly of society and holding those responsible for their heinous crimes.

Shannon Paulk, age 11, disappeared on the evening of September 1, 2001, while heading to a friend's home in Prattville, Alabama. Her disappearance signaled the start of a nightmare for the neighborhood. Despite extensive searches and investigations by law enforcement, her whereabouts remained unknown for months, leaving her family and the community gripped with fear and uncertainty.

In December 2001, a grim discovery shattered any lingering hope of Shannon's safe return when hunters stumbled upon her remains in a wooded area near Prattville, miles away from where she was last seen. The discovery of S annon's body sent shockwaves through the community, intensifying the urgency to find her killer and bring them to justice. However, despite this crucial development, the mystery surrounding Shannon's disappearance and murder only deepened, fueling speculation and raising questions about the circumstances surrounding her tragic fate.

Despite exhaustive efforts by law enforcement agencies, including the FBI, to unravel the mystery of Shannon Paulk's disappearance and murder, no substantial leads or suspects have emerged. The absence of con rete evidence and witnesses has presented a formidable challenge, thwarting attempts to bring closure to Shannon's family and the community.

The investigation into Shannon Paulk's disappearance uncovered unsettling connections to a trailer park known as Candlestick Park, which had garnered a reputation for illicit activities, including the production of X-rated movies and instances of sexual exploitation. In particular, attention was drawn to a resident known as the Halloween Man, who allegedly lured children with promises of candy and treats. It was noted that Shannon's baby walker was discovered in front of his trailer, raising suspicions about potential links to her abduction.

Furthermore, the geographical proximity of Candlestick Park to areas known for pedophile activity heightened concerns about the existence of a broader network of child exploitation within the community. These unsettling connections underscore the urgency of further investigation into the possible involvement of a pedophile ring operating within the trailer park and its potential connection to Shannon's disappearance.

The parallels between Shannon Paulk's case and others associated with pedophile rings are deeply troubling. Patterns of abduct on, grooming, and, ultimately, murder echo the modus operandi commonly observed in cases linked to child trafficking and exploitation networks. The alignment of the tactics employed in Shannon's abduction with those utilized by individuals involved in such sinister activities underscores the need for a thorough investigation into the potential involvement of a pedophile ring. Recognizing these similarities sheds light on the pervasive threat such criminal networks pose. It emphasizes the importance of swift and comprehensive action to bring perpetrators to justice and prevent further harm to innocent victims.

The stagnant state of Shannon's case, despite allocating significant resources and extensive investigative endeavors, hints at potential obstruction or interference by influential individuals or groups. The reluctance of witnesses to step forward or share vital information underscores the pervasive fear or coercion exerted by those associated with the pedophile ring. This chilling real ty highlights law enforcement agencies' formidable challenges in unraveling the complexities of cases involving powerful perpetrators. It underscores the urgent need for concerted efforts to break through the barriers of silence and bring justice to Shannon and other victims of child exploitation.

The Shannon Paulk cold case represents a tragic, unresolved mystery that haunts her family and the Prattville community. While the investigation into her disappearance and murder has faced numerous challenges, including a lack of leads and evidence, we believe that exploring the possibility of links to a pedophile ring is warranted. By shining a light on this overlooked aspect of the case, we hope to raise awareness and encourage renewed efforts to uncover the truth behind Shannon's untimely death. Only through persi tent investigation, community vigilance, and dedication to justice can we honor Shannon's memory and bring closure to her family.

David and I were deeply troubled after discussing the Shannon Paulk case, especially considering the staggering statistics surrounding child sexual abuse. It's alarming to think about the sheer number of victims in the United States alone, with millions of adults having survived such trauma. David pointed out hat the majority of sex offenders are male, and girls are disproportionately targeted, with children with disabilities at even higher risk. We also discussed the rate of re-arrest among released child molesters, highlighting the need for better prevention and intervention measures. The fact that there are over 500,000 active predators online every day, including on social media platforms, adds another layer of urgency to this issue. As parents, we feel a responsibility to educate ourselves and our children about the dangers of sexual abuse and how to stay safe. It's heartbreaking to think about the long-lasting effects of abuse on children, from low self-esteem and depression to mistrust of adults and even suicidal thoughts. We agreed that protecting our children from such harm is paramount, starting with being informed and vigilant.

Exploring the Nexus of Missing Persons and Satanic Ritual Abuse

The staggering statistics of missing persons in the United States, coupled with the grim reality that many never return, paint a haunting portrait of a pervasive and unresolved societal issue. Among the most vulnerable are children, who disappear at an alarming rate, with over 800,000 reported missing each year and an additional 500,000 going unreported. Tragically, a significant number of these missing individuals remain unaccounted for, their fates shrouded in mystery and fear. Amidst this unsettling backdrop, the specter of Satanic ritual abuse looms as a sinister possibility, raising chilling questions about the dark underbelly of society and the fate of those who vanish without a trace.

While missing person cases have long been a concern for law enforcement and communities, the phenomenon of Satanic ritual abuse introduces a macabre element of horror and intrigue. Reports and allegations of ritualistic practices involving human sacrifice, sexual abuse, and occult rituals have circulated for decades, sparking controversy and debate within both academic and law enforcement circles. Despite the sensationalized nature of some claims, there exists a disturbingly persistent pattern of allegations, suggesting that Satanic ritual abuse may not be a mere myth but a hidden reality lurking in the shadows.

The concept of Satanic ritual abuse gained widespread attention in the 1980s and 1990s, fueled by sensational media coverage and high-profile cases such as the McMartin preschool trial. While skepticism and skepticism surrounded many of these allegations, some cases revealed disturbing evidence of ritualistic practices and systematic abuse, leaving investigators grappling with the complexities of uncovering and prosecuting these crimes.

In recent years, renewed interest in the phenomenon of Satanic ritual abuse has emerged, fueled in part by advancements in forensic technology and a growing awareness of the prevalence of human trafficking and exploitation. While the exact extent of Satanic ritual abuse remains difficult to quantify due to the clandestine nature of these practices and the reluctance of victims to come forward, there is a growing recognition that such violations may be more widespread than previously acknowledged.

In light of these developments, it is essential to examine the intersection between unresolved missing persons cases and the shadow of Satanic ritual abuse. Are there patterns or connections that suggest a link between these two phenomena? What role, if any, does Satanic ritual abuse play in the disappearance and exploitation of vulnerable individuals? By delving into these questions, we may uncover new insights into the dark forces at play in our society and shed light on the plight of those who have vanished into the abyss.

Each year, approximately 630,000 people are reported missing in the United States. While the majority are eventually located, a haunting reality remains: around 90,000 individuals vanish without a trace, leaving behind shattered families and unanswered questions. The reasons for their disappearances vary, ranging from abduction and human trafficking to mental health crises and voluntary disappearances. However, for a subset of the missing, the possibility of falling victim to Satanic ritual abuse casts a chilling shadow over their fate.

For those who disappear without a trace, the journey into the abyss of the unknown is fraught with uncertainty and fear. Families are left to grapple with the unbearable uncertainty of not knowing whether their loved ones are alive or dead, safe or suffering. Every missed birthday, holiday, and milestone serves as a painful reminder of their absence, perpetuating a cycle of grief and anguish.

The reasons behind these disappearances are as varied as the individuals themselves. Strangers abduct some, lured away by promises of love or opportunity, only to be trapped in the clutches of human traffickers or predators. Others succumb to mental health crises, wandering off in a state of confusion or distress, their whereabouts remaining a mystery to all who know them.

In some cases, individuals choose to disappear voluntarily, seeking refuge from trauma, abuse, or perceived threats. While a desire for escape or self-preservation may drive their decision, the consequences are often devastating, leaving behind a trail of heartache and uncertainty for their loved ones.

Amidst this complex landscape of disappearances, the specter of Satanic ritual abuse emerges as a chilling possibility, casting a shadow over the fate of those who vanish without a trace. Reports and allegations of ritualistic practices involving human sacrifice, sexual abuse, and occult rituals raise disturbing questions about the hidden dangers lurking in the shadows of society.

While skepticism surrounds many claims of Satanic ritual abuse, there exists a persistent pattern of allegations that cannot be ignored. The prevalence of such practices remains difficult to quantify, given the clandestine nature of these crimes and the reluctance of victims to come forward. Yet, the possibility that some of the missing may have fallen victim to these dark forces cannot be dismissed lightly.

As we confront the grim reality of the missing, it is essential to acknowledge the multifaceted nature of their plight. Whether abducted by predators, lost to mental illness, or trapped in the web of Satanic ritual abuse, each missing person represents a tragedy that reverberates through their families and communities. It is incumbent upon us to shine a light into the darkness, to search for answers, and to hold those responsible for these crimes accountable. Only then can we begin to bring closure to the families of the missing and prevent future tragedies from befalling others.

Satanic ritual abuse refers to a heinous form of abuse and torture perpetrated within the context of Satanic rituals. While cases of Satanic ritual abuse are rare and often contested, survivors' accounts paint a disturbing picture of ritualistic ceremonies involving torture, sexual abuse, and psychological manipulation. Victims, usually children or vulnerable individuals, are subjected to unspeakable horrors orchestrated by individuals or groups steeped in Satanic beliefs or ideologies. The secrecy surrounding these rituals, coupled with the manipulation and coercion tactics employed by perpetrators, makes detection and prosecution challenging, leaving many cases unresolved.

At the heart of Satanic ritual abuse lies a disturbing intersection of violence, exploitation, and belief systems that defy comprehension. Survivors' testimonies offer glimpses into the nightmarish world of ritualistic ceremonies, where innocent victims are subjected to unimaginable acts of cruelty in the name of Satanic worship. These ceremonies often involve elements of torture, sexual abuse, and psychological torment, leaving lasting scars on the bodies and minds of those who endure them.

Children are particularly vulnerable to Satanic ritual abuse, as perpetrators often target the young and defenseless for their nefarious purposes. Manipulated and coerced into participating in rituals they cannot comprehend, these innocent victims suffer in silence, their voices drowned out by the darkness that surrounds them. For many survivors, the trauma of Satanic ritual abuse casts a long shadow over their lives, shaping their identities and relationships in profound and lasting ways.

The secrecy surrounding Satanic ritual abuse poses significant challenges for law enforcement and legal authorities tasked with investigating and prosecuting these crimes. Perpetrators operate within tightly-knit groups, shielded from scrutiny by secrecy and deception. Victims, too, are often silenced through threats and intimidation, making it difficult for them to come forward and seek justice for the horrors they have endured.

Despite these challenges, efforts to raise awareness about Satanic ritual abuse and support survivors have gained traction in recent years. Advocacy groups, mental health professionals, and law enforcement agencies are working together to shed light on this dark phenomenon and provide much-needed support to those affected by it. By amplifying survivors' voices, raising public awareness, and holding perpetrators accountable, we can begin to confront the scourge of Satanic ritual abuse and ensure that victims receive the justice and support they deserve.

In confronting the reality of Satanic ritual abuse, it is essential to acknowledge the profound suffering endured by survivors and the challenges they face in seeking justice and healing. By shining a light into the darkness of this hidden crime, we can empower survivors, hold perpetrators accountable, and work towards a future where no one is subjected to such unspeakable horrors in the name of ideology or belief.

The intersection of missing persons cases and Satanic ritual abuse is a chilling reality that cannot be ignored. While concrete evidence linking the two remains elusive, anecdotal accounts and survivor testimony suggest that some missing individuals may have fallen victim to these horrific practices. The clandestine nature of Satanic rituals, coupled with the vulnerabilities of missing persons, creates fertile ground for exploitation and abuse. Tragically, the lack of resolution in many missing persons cases leaves open the possibility that some may have met a fate far more sinister than initially imagined.

The connection between missing persons cases and Satanic ritual abuse underscores the complexity and darkness that permeates these phenomena. For families searching for their loved ones, the possibility that their absence may be linked to Satanic rituals adds a layer of horror and uncertainty to their already agonizing ordeal. While definitive proof may be lacking, the parallels between the circumstances of some missing persons and the modus operandi of Satanic ritual abusers cannot be dismissed outright.

Survivor testimonies provide haunting glimpses into the intersection of missing persons and Satanic ritual abuse, recounting experiences of abduction, captivity, and unspeakable torture at the hands of perpetrators steeped in Satanic beliefs. For these individuals, the line between missing persons and victims of ritual abuse blurs as they navigate the harrowing journey of survival and recovery in the aftermath of unimaginable trauma.

The clandestine nature of Satanic ritual abuse complicates efforts to uncover the truth behind missing persons cases linked to these practices. Perpetrators operate within secretive networks, shielded from scrutiny by deception and intimidation. Victims, too, may be silenced through threats and coercion, making it difficult for them to come forward and disclose their experiences.

Despite these challenges, efforts to shed light on the nexus between missing persons and Satanic ritual abuse are underway. Advocacy groups, law enforcement agencies, and mental health professionals are working to raise awareness about the prevalence of ritual abuse and provide support to survivors. By amplifying survivor voices, conducting thorough investigations, and addressing the systemic factors that enable these crimes, we can begin to unravel the tangled web of darkness that ensnares missing persons and victims of Satanic ritual abuse alike.

In confronting the nexus between missing persons and Satanic ritual abuse, it is essential to acknowledge the profound impact on survivors and their families. By recognizing their experiences and supporting their journey to healing and justice, we can honor the resilience and courage of those who have endured unimaginable suffering. Together, we must shine a light into the shadows, illuminating the truth and working towards a future where no one is lost to the darkness of Satanic ritual abuse.

The plight of missing persons, coupled with the specter of Satanic ritual abuse, demands urgent attention and action. Efforts to enhance public awareness, improve reporting mechanisms, and strengthen support systems for survivors are essential steps in addressing this multifaceted crisis. Additionally, law enforcement agencies must prioritize the investigation and resolution of missing persons cases, including those with potential ties to ritualistic abuse. Collaboration between law enforcement, mental health professionals, and victim advocacy groups is paramount in providing comprehensive support to survivors and their families.

The epidemic of unresolved missing persons cases in the United States, juxtaposed with the disturbing specter of Satanic ritual abuse, underscores the urgent need for concerted action. As a society, we must confront the uncomfortable realities of exploitation and abuse that lurk in the shadows, shining a light on the darkness that threatens the most vulnerable among us. By raising awareness, enhancing support systems, and prioritizing the investigation and resolution of missing persons cases, we can strive towards a future where everyone is valued, protected, and accounted for.

To effectively address the crisis of missing persons and Satanic ritual abuse, a multifaceted approach is necessary, involving both preventative and responsive measures. Educating the public about the prevalence of missing person cases and the signs of Satanic ritual abuse is crucial in empowering individuals to recognize and report suspicious activities. Public awareness campaigns through various media channels, educational institutions, and community organizations can help disseminate information and dispel myths surrounding these issues.

Improving reporting mechanisms for cases of missing persons, including the establishment of dedicated hotlines and online platforms, can facilitate timely and efficient responses from law enforcement agencies. Encouraging prompt reporting and supporting individuals who come forward with information is essential in increasing the chances of locating missing individuals and apprehending perpetrators. Enhancing support services for survivors of Satanic ritual abuse and their families is critical in aiding their recovery and healing process. This includes access to trauma-informed counseling, legal advocacy, medical assistance, and safe housing options.

Collaborating with mental health professionals, victim advocacy groups, and faith-based organizations can ensure comprehensive support for survivors and their loved ones. Fostering collaboration between law enforcement agencies at the local, state, and federal levels is essential in coordinating efforts to investigate and prosecute cases of missing persons and Satanic ritual abuse. Interagency task forces that address these issues can streamline information sharing, resource allocation, and joint investigative efforts, leading to more effective outcomes. Engaging communities in prevention and intervention efforts is crucial in building trust, fostering collaboration, and mobilizing collective action against exploitation and abuse. Community-based initiatives, such as neighborhood watch programs, youth outreach campaigns, and faith-based initiatives, can empower individuals to play an active role in safeguarding vulnerable populations and raising awareness about the realities of missing persons and Satanic ritual abuse.

By implementing these strategies and mobilizing resources at the local, regional, and national levels, we can work towards addressing the crisis of missing persons and Satanic ritual abuse, ensuring that every individual is protected, supported, and accounted for. Through collective action and unwavering commitment, we can strive for a future where exploitation and abuse are eradicated and all individuals can live free from fear and oppression.

Guide to Allegations of Ritual and Child Abuse

During the 1950s and 1960s, discussions surrounding child sexual abuse primarily focused on the "stranger danger" concept, depicting perpetrators as sinister individuals preying on innocent children. This simplistic narrative was perpetuated by posters and campaigns warning children to avoid gifts and rides from strangers. However, as our understanding of child sexual abuse evolved, it became clear that perpetrators could be anyone, including individuals known and trusted by the child.

The myth of the child victim as purely innocent and the offender as purely evil has been challenged, particularly in cases involving child sex rings and child prostitution. Society's discomfort with victims who do not fit the stereotype of innocence and offenders who do not fit the stereotype of evil complicates discussions around sexual abuse prevention and intervention.

In the 1970s, the focus shifted towards recognizing intrafamilial child sexual abuse, particularly incestuous relationships involving relatives known to the child. However, this narrow focus on father-daughter incest overshadowed other forms of abuse, perpetuating the misconception that child sexual abuse only occurs within families.

In the 1980s, concerns about missing children reignited discussions around "stranger danger," leading to heightened fears of stranger abductions. However, this narrative often overlooked other forms of child victimization, such as acquaintance molestation, where perpetrators are individuals known to the child.

Acquaintance molestation, including cases involving trusted figures like priests, neighbors, and scout leaders, has been a problematic aspect of child sexual abuse for society to confront. Prevention programs emphasizing "say no, yell, and tell" may inadvertently contribute to victim guilt and self-blame in cases where children are manipulated or groomed by perpetrators.

In recent years, the narrative of "stranger danger" has resurfaced in discussions around satanic ritual abuse, attributing child victimization to devil-worshipping cults. However, data suggests that such cases are rare, and exaggerated claims have undermined efforts to address the reality of child sexual abuse.

Overall, the evolution of societal attitudes towards child sexual abuse highlights the need for nuanced approaches to prevention and intervention, recognizing the complexity of perpetrators and victims involved.

The terms "satanic," "occult," and "ritual" are often used interchangeably, yet their precise definitions remain elusive. While some may define satanism based on their religious beliefs, others may attribute the label to any belief system outside their own. The concept of ritual is similarly complex, encompassing religious ceremonies, cultural customs, and repetitive behaviors driven by psychological or sexual needs.

In law enforcement training, discussions often center around satanic ritual abuse, witchcraft, and occult practices, though these may not always align with traditional satanism. Instead, they may involve cultural or spiritual rituals unrelated to satanic belief systems. Furthermore, the presence of ritualistic elements does not necessarily indicate criminal activity.

The term "ritual child abuse" is fraught with ambiguity and may not accurately capture the complexities of abuse cases involving spiritual indoctrination. Differentiating between satanic and non-satanic abuse based on specific symbols or rituals presents challenges, as many rituals have cultural or religious significance beyond satanism.

Crime scenes featuring symbols or acts commonly associated with satanism or the occult may not always indicate genuine belief or affiliation with such ideologies. Bizarre or cruel crimes, while disturbing, do not inherently signify satanic involvement. Similarly, crimes committed on dates considered significant in satanic or occult traditions may lack genuine spiritual motivation.

The proliferation of misinformation and varying interpretations of symbols and dates associated with satanic practices further complicates the identification of satanic or occult crimes. Handouts and training materials often lack verifiable sources, leading to the widespread dissemination of unverified information within law enforcement circles.

In the early 1980s, law enforcement agencies began encountering cases involving allegations of child sexual abuse characterized by multiple young victims, multiple offenders, fear as a controlling tactic, and bizarre or ritualistic activity. These cases, which I refer to as multidimensional child sex rings, presented significant challenges in investigation and prosecution.

Common characteristics of these cases include the involvement of both male and female offenders. These situational molesters may not have a proper sexual preference for children, male and female victims targeted from birth to six years old, and motivations beyond sexual gratification, possibly rooted in anger, hostility, or spiritual beliefs.

These cases often emerge from scenarios such as adult survivors seeking therapy and recalling childhood victimization, daycare cases involving multiple victims and staff members, abuse within families or isolated neighborhoods, and allegations arising from custody or visitation disputes.

Victims of multidimensional child sex rings allege a range of activities, including human sacrifice, cannibalism, and vampirism, some of which seem physically impossible or improbable. Despite extensive investigations, the bodies of alleged murder victims have never been found.

The term "ritual abuse" or "satanic ritual abuse" has been used to describe these cases, but such terminology may imply specific motivations that are not universally present. It remains challenging to accurately define and understand the dynamics of multidimensional child sex rings, requiring ongoing research and investigation.

In the realm of criminal investigation, few topics are as emotionally charged and intellectually perplexing as the alleged existence of multidimensional child sex rings. At the intersection of societal fears, forensic science, and human psychology lies a labyrinth of claims, counterclaims, and deeply ingrained beliefs. This paper delves into the intricate web of allegations, examining the challenges law enforcement agencies face, the complexities of victim statements, and the blurred line between reality and myth.

The specter of multidimensional child sex rings looms large in the collective consciousness, fueled by sensational media coverage, urban legends, and historical anxieties. Yet, amidst the cacophony of voices, the quest for truth remains elusive. This paper embarks on a journey to untangle the threads of truth from the fabric of myth, shedding light on the nuances of investigation, victim testimony, and the enduring allure of conspiracy theories.

Central to the investigation of alleged multidimensional child sex rings are the formidable challenges faced by law enforcement agencies. Unlike conventional crimes with tangible evidence and identifiable suspects, these cases often unfold in a shadowy realm where deception and manipulation obscure truth. The absence of physical evidence compounds the difficulty, leaving investigators to navigate a maze of testimonies, conjectures, and competing narratives.

At the heart of the matter lie the testimonies of alleged victims, whose accounts serve as both the investigation's cornerstone and quagmire. While every disclosure demands scrutiny and empathy, distinguishing fact from fiction poses a Herculean task. The passage of time, the influence of external parties, and the trauma experienced by the victims all cast doubt upon the veracity of their claims. Yet, within the labyrinth of memory and trauma, fragments of truth may lie waiting to be unearthed.

Embedded within the discourse surrounding alleged multidimensional child sex rings is a complex tapestry of human psychology, belief systems, and societal fears. From the allure of conspiracy theories to the power of suggestion, the human mind is a fertile ground for the proliferation of myths and legends. Investigators must navigate the murky waters of belief, skepticism, and cognitive bias as they grapple with competing narratives.

In the pursuit of justice, the investigation of alleged multidimensional child sex rings demands not only diligence and expertise but also a nuanced understanding of human behavior and societal dynamics. As we navigate the labyrinth of claims and counterclaims, let us not lose sight of the humanity at the heart of the matter—the victims whose voices cry out for justice and the perpetrators whose deeds shroud them in darkness. In the end, we can only hope to uncover the truth hidden within by shedding light on the shadows of myth and misconception.

Facts About Satanic Ritual Abuse

Satanic Ritual Abuse (SRA) is a deeply controversial and highly secretive phenomenon that has elicited fear, skepticism, and vehement denial within society. Despite its contentious nature, it is imperative to approach the topic with objectivity and sensitivity, acknowledging the gravity of the issue and the need for careful verification procedures.

The reality of SRA is shrouded in secrecy, making it challenging to discuss without facing vilification and skepticism. However, dismissing it outright would be a disservice to the victims who have come forward with their experiences of abuse and exploitation.

Law enforcement agencies are often confronted with the daunting task of recognizing and addressing instances of SRA, which may involve clandestine networks and self-appointed leaders operating outside the bounds of legal and ethical norms. Training for law enforcement personnel is essential to ensure that they can effectively identify and respond to cases of SRA, prioritizing the safety and well-being of those affected.

The origins of the controversy surrounding SRA can be traced back to the so-called "satanic panic" of the late 20th century, during which allegations of widespread cult activity and ritual abuse captivated cultural, religious, and law enforcement communities. However, distinguishing between genuine accounts of abuse and false allegations requires scrutiny and forensic analysis, particularly given the susceptibility of vulnerable individuals to coercion and manipulation.

The portrayal of SRA in media, both traditional and social, has contributed to the perpetuation of moral panics and sensationalized narratives, often resulting in unjust consequences for individuals falsely accused of involvement in cult activities. The impact of these false accusations extends beyond the immediate victims to their families, communities, and therapists, highlighting the need for responsible reporting and evidence-based investigations.

Victims of SRA experience profound psychological, social, and economic harm, similar to other victims of interpersonal violence. Shame, self-blame, and isolation compound their vulnerability, making it imperative to provide support and treatment to those who come forward with their experiences. Believing survivors and offering them the necessary resources for healing and recovery is essential to addressing the complex trauma associated with SRA.

Despite the lack of scientific evidence supporting large-scale SRA networks, belief in its prevalence persists among specific segments of society. This belief can have far-reaching consequences, influencing the treatment of individuals accused of perpetrating ritual abuse and perpetuating unfounded witch hunts against innocent individuals.

The phenomenon of Satanic Ritual Abuse is a complex and contentious issue that demands careful consideration and compassionate response. By acknowledging the experiences of survivors, providing support and resources, and conducting thorough and evidence-based investigations, we can work towards addressing the underlying issues of abuse and exploitation while upholding the principles of justice and integrity within our communities.

Understanding and Combating Child Sex Trafficking

Child sex trafficking lurks in the shadows of society, a pervasive and sinister crime that inflicts unimaginable harm on its victims and stains the moral fabric of our communities. In this chapter, we embark on a journey to explore the depths of this crisis, shedding light on its magnitude and far-reaching consequences.

Conservative estimates paint a grim picture, suggesting that up to 500,000 children are ensnared in sex trafficking each day. However, the true number may exceed a staggering 1.2 million, underscoring the urgent need for action to combat this heinous crime.

Child sex trafficking is not a standalone issue but rather a complex web of interconnected factors. Economic disparities, social vulnerabilities, lack of education, political instability, and systemic inequalities all render children susceptible to exploitation and trafficking. The rise of digital platforms and the anonymity of the internet have further facilitated the growth of online trafficking networks, exacerbating the crisis.

The repercussions of child sex trafficking are profound and enduring. Beyond the physical and sexual abuse endured, survivors often grapple with severe psychological trauma, including PTSD, depression, and anxiety. Many face stigma and social alienation, hindering their reintegration into society. Moreover, the cycle of exploitation perpetuates intergenerational poverty and vulnerability, ensnaring victims in a cycle of despair.

The consequences of child sex trafficking extend far beyond individual victims, permeating society at large. It violates the fundamental rights and dignity of children, corrodes social trust, and undermines community morals. Additionally, the economic costs of trafficking impose a heavy toll on society, including healthcare expenses, law enforcement efforts, and lost productivity.

Child sex trafficking presents a grave and pressing crisis that demands collective attention and action. By comprehending the scale of the problem, addressing its root causes, and providing comprehensive support to survivors, we can strive to eradicate this abhorrent crime and foster a safer, more equitable world for all children.

Efforts to combat child sex trafficking have seen progress through legal amendments and prevention initiatives. Awareness and education are pivotal in identifying victims and addressing the social determinants of health related to trafficking. Major institutions, organizations, and cybersecurity firms play a crucial role in research, advocacy, and law enforcement efforts.

Survivors of child sex trafficking face numerous obstacles in their journey to heal and recover. A well-funded service and shelter array, tailored to their needs, is essential for their rehabilitation and empowerment. Community participation, anticipatory thinking, and informed resource allocation are key in establishing effective support systems for survivors.

As we confront the shadows of child sex trafficking, let us stand united in our resolve to protect the most vulnerable among us. Through knowledge, advocacy, and concerted action, we can dismantle the networks of exploitation and create a future where every child is safe, valued, and free from harm.

Factors Contributing to Underreporting of Child Sex Trafficking

The underreporting of child sex trafficking represents a critical challenge in addressing this pervasive crime and providing support to its victims. This section explores the profound consequences of underreporting, highlighting how it perpetuates exploitation, delays justice, and exacerbates the trauma experienced by survivors.

Despite the pervasive nature of child sex trafficking, the actual number of reported cases often fails to reflect the accurate scale of the problem. This paper examines the factors contributing to underreporting, shedding light on the barriers preventing victims from seeking help and authorities from effectively combating this crime.

Victims of child sex trafficking are often subjected to coercion, threats, and physical violence by their traffickers, instilling a profound sense of fear and intimidation. The threat of retaliation against themselves or their loved ones looms large, preventing victims from coming forward or seeking assistance. Traffickers may employ tactics such as blackmail, manipulation, and isolation to maintain control over their victims, perpetuating a cycle of abuse and silence.

The stigma associated with being a victim of sex trafficking can be overwhelming, leading survivors to internalize feelings of shame and self-blame. Society's pervasive misconceptions and victim-blaming attitudes further exacerbate these feelings, making it difficult for survivors to disclose their exploitation. Many victims fear judgment, rejection, and social ostracization, leading them to suffer in silence rather than face the stigma associated with being a "trafficked person."

Victims of child sex trafficking often harbor deep-seated mistrust towards law enforcement and other authority figures. Past negative experiences or perceptions of institutional betrayal may erode victims' confidence in the justice system, hindering their willingness to report their exploitation. Moreover, the fear of retribution or deportation, particularly among undocumented victims, further exacerbates this lack of trust and inhibits victims from seeking help or cooperating with law enforcement.

Despite increased efforts to raise awareness about human trafficking, many individuals, including potential victims and bystanders, remain unaware of the signs and indicators of trafficking. Victims may not recognize their exploitation as trafficking due to manipulation or coercion by their traffickers. At the same time, bystanders may fail to intervene or report suspicious activities due to ignorance or indifference. Furthermore, the lack of accessible information and resources on how to report trafficking incidents further contributes to underreporting and perpetuates a culture of silence.

The underreporting of child sex trafficking represents a significant obstacle in efforts to combat this heinous crime and provide support to its victims. By understanding the complex interplay of factors contributing to underreporting, stakeholders can develop more targeted interventions and strategies to overcome these barriers. Empowering victims to break the cycle of silence, reducing stigma and shame, building trust with marginalized communities, and increasing awareness and education are critical steps toward addressing underreporting and ensuring that survivors receive the assistance and justice they deserve.

When cases of child sex trafficking go unreported, traffickers are encouraged to continue their exploitation unchecked. The absence of accountability and consequences enables traffickers to maintain control over their victims, perpetuating cycles of abuse and exploitation. Victims remain trapped in situations of coercion and violence, unable to escape or seek assistance without the fear of reprisal. Thus, underreporting not only prolongs the suffering of current victims but also puts countless others at risk of falling prey to traffickers in the future.

Cases of child sex trafficking that are reported years or even decades after the abuse occurs present significant challenges for investigators and law enforcement agencies. Evidence may deteriorate over time, witnesses may become unavailable or unreliable, and victims' memories may fade or become fragmented. As a result, pursuing justice becomes increasingly complex, and perpetrators may evade accountability for their crimes. Delayed justice not only denies survivors the closure and validation they deserve but also undermines efforts to hold traffickers accountable and prevent future exploitation.

The failure to report instances of child sex trafficking perpetuates the trauma experienced by survivors, prolonging their suffering and impeding their healing process. Without acknowledgment and validation of their experiences, victims may struggle to come to terms with the abuse they endured. They may be unable to access the support and resources they need to recover. The psychological toll of unaddressed trauma can be profound, leading to long-term mental health issues such as PTSD, depression, and anxiety. Moreover, the lack of acknowledgment may further isolate survivors, exacerbating feelings of shame, self-blame, and worthlessness.

Effectively combating child sex trafficking requires proactive measures to address the pervasive issue of underreporting. This section explores key strategies to increase awareness, enhance victim support services, and strengthen legal protections to encourage reporting and provide comprehensive care for survivors.

Comprehensive education and awareness campaigns play a pivotal role in empowering individuals to recognize the signs of trafficking and take action to report suspicious activity. These campaigns should target diverse audiences, including children, parents, educators, healthcare professionals, law enforcement agencies, and community members. By providing information on the tactics used by traffickers, the vulnerabilities of potential victims, and the avenues for reporting trafficking incidents, these initiatives can mobilize communities to become vigilant allies in the fight against exploitation.

Accessible and trauma-informed support services are essential to encourage victims to come forward and provide them with the comprehensive care they need to heal and rebuild their lives. This includes specialized counseling, medical assistance, housing, legal advocacy, and case management services tailored to the unique needs of trafficking survivors. By prioritizing survivors' autonomy, dignity, and safety, these services can create a supportive environment where victims feel empowered to seek help and engage with law enforcement without fear of retribution or judgment.

Legal reforms and policies that prioritize victim protection and support are critical in encouraging reporting and facilitating prosecutions against traffickers. This includes enacting legislation that criminalizes all forms of trafficking and provides robust penalties for perpetrators, as well as establishing mechanisms for the identification and protection of victims. Moreover, legal protections should encompass provisions for victim assistance, including access to legal representation, immigration relief, and compensation for damages. By enhancing legal protections for survivors and holding traffickers accountable for their crimes, these measures can create a more enabling environment for reporting and prosecuting trafficking cases.

The consequences of underreporting in child sex trafficking are far-reaching and devastating, perpetuating cycles of exploitation, delaying justice, and prolonging the trauma experienced by survivors. Addressing underreporting requires a multifaceted approach that empowers victims to come forward, builds trust with marginalized communities, enhances awareness and education, and strengthens support services for survivors. By breaking the cycle of silence and holding perpetrators accountable, we can work towards creating a safer and more just society for all children.

Addressing underreporting in child sex trafficking requires a holistic approach that combines efforts to increase awareness, enhance victim support services, and strengthen legal protections. By empowering individuals to recognize and report trafficking, providing survivors with the support they need to heal and seek justice, and implementing legal reforms that prioritize victim rights, we can work towards dismantling the culture of silence and impunity that enables exploitation to thrive. Together, we can create a future where all children are safe, protected, and free from the scourge of trafficking.

The Disturbing Reality of Child Sex Trafficking: Exploitation in Unexpected Places

Child sex trafficking represents a grave threat to the safety and well-being of children, with traffickers often exploiting innocence and trust in seemingly safe environments. This paper explores the disturbing reality of how traffickers recruit victims from unexpected places, such as Boys and Girls Clubs and churches, and the urgent need for awareness and vigilance in protecting children from exploitation.

Traffickers prey upon the trust and goodwill of communities by infiltrating trusted institutions, such as community centers and religious organizations. By posing as mentors, volunteers, or even fellow members of the community, traffickers gain access to vulnerable children and establish a facade of credibility and legitimacy. This deception not only facilitates the recruitment process but also undermines the perception of these institutions as safe havens for children, perpetuating a sense of betrayal and disillusionment.

Traffickers entice children with false promises of love, attention, and opportunity, preying upon their innate desires for affection, acceptance, and a better future. These promises may take various forms, including offers of affectionate relationships, glamorous lifestyles, or lucrative employment opportunities. By exploiting children's vulnerabilities and aspirations, traffickers manipulate them into compliance, effectively grooming them for exploitation without their awareness or consent.

Once ensnared, traffickers employ a range of psychological manipulation and coercion tactics to exert control over their victims. These tactics may include threats of violence, isolation from family and friends, and psychological manipulation aimed at instilling fear, dependency, and obedience. Traffickers exploit children's vulnerabilities, making them feel powerless to resist and trapping them in situations of exploitation from which escape seems impossible.

The recruitment of children from unexpected places, such as Boys and Girls Clubs and churches, underscores the insidious nature of child sex trafficking and the urgent need for awareness and vigilance in protecting children from exploitation. By understanding the tactics used by traffickers to prey upon innocence and trust, communities can work together to strengthen safeguards, raise awareness, and empower children to recognize and resist exploitation. Together, we can create a safer and more resilient environment where all children are valued, protected, and free from the scourge of trafficking.

The Franklin Child Prostitution Ring Allegations

The Franklin child prostitution ring allegations that emerged in June 1988 in Omaha, Nebraska, sent shockwaves through the community and reverberated across the nation. This paper delves into the disturbing events surrounding the allegations, examining the accusations against prominent Nebraska political and business figures, the subsequent investigations, and the broader implications for society. By exploring the complexities of this case, we aim to shed light on the challenges of confronting child sex trafficking and the importance of seeking justice for victims.

In June 1988, the quiet city of Omaha, Nebraska, was rocked by allegations of a child prostitution ring operating at the highest echelons of society. Accusations surfaced implicating prominent political and business figures in heinous acts of child sex trafficking. The ensuing scandal, known as the Franklin child prostitution ring allegations, exposed a dark underbelly of corruption and abuse that shocked the community and challenged the nation's conscience.

The allegations centered around the operations of a purported child prostitution ring that exploited vulnerable minors for the gratification of wealthy and influential individuals. Victims, many of whom were from disadvantaged backgrounds, came forward with harrowing accounts of abuse, coercion, and exploitation at the hands of their perpetrators—the scale and audacity of the alleged crimes sent shockwaves through Omaha and beyond.

Among those implicated in the allegations were prominent Nebraska political and business figures, including politicians, business people, and community leaders. Accusations of involvement in the child prostitution ring tarnished the reputations of individuals who held positions of trust and authority, leading to widespread disbelief and outrage.

The allegations prompted investigations by law enforcement agencies and regulatory bodies, yet the outcomes were marred by controversy and skepticism. Witness testimonies were dismissed, evidence was questioned, and allegations were often met with disbelief or outright denial. Despite mounting pressure for accountability, many of the accused individuals evaded prosecution or faced minimal consequences for their alleged actions.

The Franklin child prostitution ring allegations had far-reaching implications for society, highlighting the pervasive nature of child sex trafficking and the vulnerabilities of marginalized communities. The case exposed systemic failures in protecting vulnerable children and holding perpetrators accountable, raising questions about the integrity of institutions entrusted with safeguarding the public.

While the Franklin case remains clouded in controversy and uncertainty, the quest for justice for the victims continues. Advocates and activists tirelessly campaign for truth and accountability, demanding recognition of the survivors' experiences and accountability for those responsible for their exploitation. The Franklin claims remain a sobering reminder of the continuous effort to combat child sex trafficking and safeguard society's most vulnerable citizens.

The Franklin child prostitution ring allegations represent a dark chapter in Omaha's history and a sobering reminder of the horrors of child sex trafficking. Despite the challenges and controversies surrounding the case, seeking truth and justice for the victims is essential. By confronting the realities of exploitation and abuse, we can work towards building a society where every child is safe, protected, and free from harm.

The most important problem concerning the Franklin case is piecing together exactly what happened. The most thorough investigation of the affair is that of John DeCamp, the attorney who became slightly famous in anthropology and sociology, given his book about the Franklin case and his efforts to promote the case. "Nebraskagate," a term DeCamp uses to describe the Franklin allegations and their cover-up, exemplifies many themes concerning the media and the problem of possibly missing accounts. For example, DeCamp is sharp in his criticisms of the American press and points out its bias against marginal stories, particularly those of abuse cases. DeCamp conveniently classified the allegations of child abuse as a case of "tawdry tabloid journalism." Assails journalists for failing to investigate the sordid tale of evil and accuses them of ignoring seemingly credible testimony and witnesses.

Furthermore, the Nebraskagate book is replete with quotes offering actions that point to some conspiracy to keep pedophilia allegations quiet. Finally, the Nebraskagate account highlights cultural conflicts involving Nebraska's "husker heartland." The cultural tensions concern not just the false claims of child abuse but also racism and class issues.

The Franklin child prostitution ring: Controversies and Conspiracy Theories. This paper aims to give an overview of what is known and what remains controversial surrounding the Franklin child prostitution and abuse allegations. It is organized around what I view as the most significant controversies that linger from the Franklin affair. In addition, in the last section of the paper, I review some conspiracy theories concerning the affair and discuss some evidence from the Franklin case that may permit one to evaluate these theories critically.

In November 1989, the Nebraska State Foster Care Review Board prepared a report on institutional child abuse. One review board staff tried to draw public attention to the report and took it to John DeCamp, a lawyer and former state senator. She was fired when she refused to give up her job and filed a suit claiming stress. When DeCamp attempted to call attention to the report, he was targeted by accusations of child molestation from a woman who was later revealed to have been diagnosed with severe psychiatric disorders. Several grand juries were dismissed after their appointed judge examined the alleged charges and concluded that the accused men were themselves victims of "a carefully crafted campaign of misinformation by a sincerely concerned group of individuals." The Nebraska Foster Care Review Board report is marked confidential and had not been addressed during his trial. In 1999, federal judge Warren Urbom ordered Lawrence E. King to pay $1 million in compensatory damages and $1,000,000 in punitive damages for his association with the reported offenses against Alicia Owen.

At the same time as the investigation was unfolding, John DeCamp, a Nebraska state senator actively involved in the case, began writing letters to officials nationwide to draw public and political attention to the situation and his belief that a high-level cover-up was sabotaging the investigation. The public disclosure of the alleged events outside the investigation and legal proceedings would plant further seeds of mystery and terror around the story. Paul Bonacci, a victim of the alleged abuses, filed a lawsuit against Lawrence E. King, alleging that King and influential political associates had forced him to participate in several of the described activities. King never appeared in court for any of the proceedings, and in 1999, due to Bonacci's having suffered a default judgment, ordered him to pay a total of $800,000 to his alleged victim. John DeCamp, as a representative of the private investigative firm The Schmidt List, also began seeking independently verifiable evidence for some of the more outrageous allegations being made by the victims, many of which dated far back in time and whose details might have proven impossible to remember accurately. The Metropolitan Bureau of Investigation in Florida confiscated a load of toys headed for the Republican Convention to be donated to people experiencing poverty in a ceremony arranged by the White House. Such is the collage of hyperreality created. However, unlike in the case of the Menendez case or the multi-victim Satanic abuse cases, the Franklin case refuses to go away. It lies in bed, ready to spring up anytime and demand attention.

However, the Senator committee in Nebraska launched a probe to know why Caradori's evidence had been rejected. Senator Loran Schmit headed the legislative committee and thanked Caradori for his thorough investigative methods that managed to retrieve more victims. Three or four additional teams were sent out to interview the newly discovered victims. Caradori was also assisted by Karen Ormiston, a former police officer, and James "Tad" Armbruster, an agency State Patrol investigator on leave. In addition, on January 11 of the following year, Senator committee members Povondra, Kristensen, and Schmit announced establishing a $25,000 reward fund to come to terms with details of individuals who would have kidnapped and murdered Johnny. Charitable citizens and organizations donated the funds.

The investigation began in "late May or early June 1988" when Gary Caradori, an investigator for the Nebraska Legislature's Franklin committee, which was formed in July 1988 to examine the handling of the Franklin case by the judicial system, pursued two alleged pimps of young boys, called "E." Francis Ford, an employee of the Nebraska Foster Care Review Board, initially reported the sex ring. Caradori was accused of being overzealous in his investigative methods and of breaking rules that would secure protection from hours of investigations. Caradori was also charged with failing to inform the various authorities about how he obtained the details about the kidnappers. "E" was declared a non-credible witness, and testimonies from other victims were also rejected; one who did not deny being at sex parties contradicted evidence by Caradori's witness to the location of the house.

Two were abused in an orphanage in Omaha, border in the island of St. Thomas. The child abuse confirmed CIA investigators and alleged participants involved in the sex-drug case of the Franklin child abuse. There have been denials, however, that led to claims of a cover-up, including federal judges, victims, and witnesses. On February 14, 1990, Republican Carter White House housing and acting Bush Chief of Staff Craig Spence were called reporting that the portrait of Craig Spence claimed to receive a daily morning Washington Times. In March 1990, the eight children claimed that Peter C. Animal and Larry King would not have responded to the federal and state investigation that led to the board. At the grand jury meeting in secret two months later, there were 4,500 people seated on the grand jury in secret session; two of the children claimed themselves on that grand jury were sworn in that session. Three witnesses linked to the case were indicted on May 24, stating that period significantly impacted that presidential candidate.

In July 1989, the United States Attorney submitted an indictment to a federal Grand Jury to investigate the case. There were 29 indictments listed, embezzlement connected with the Franklin Case, leads from the original grand jury's file. The Omaha FBI office discredited evidence and witnesses, which led to the blocked efforts of legitimate state and federal investigations of the Franklin child prostitution ring, with the evidence tampering by the U.S. Attorney's office and grand jury ride. Several of the records were sealed until the mid-2013. After further closely calculated grand jury investigations, leads were blocked in 1989 to protect its present and former Republican Party incumbent and leached the Nebraska State offices.

Gunderson continues to assert that the investigation was financially dismantled and the destroyed evidence, including the missing tape recordings of the borrowed private investigator Diane Watson, the police informants, and the minor children involved, was moved to and stored off-site at the World-Herald's library. The 100 boxes of various files and sealed statements involving the scandal are now stored under court order in the secured vault of the Douglas County Courthouse in Omaha. In December 1991, a grand jury was empaneled in Douglas County, Nebraska, to consider the allegations of Lawrence E. King Jr.'s sexual abuse of Omaha youth. James Daniel McDevitt of Spokane, Washington, working with Lincoln attorney JuJu Jacobs, sued King for $1,000,000 in 1992. In 1993, McDevitt and Jacobs sued FBI informant and local child finder "Alisha Owen" for compensation.

In 1989, several hundred pages of court documents detailing the investigation of the Franklin child prostitution ring were initially set to be declassified in 2013. However, these documents were ordered to be declassified earlier in 1995. FBI Special Agent-In-Charge Theodore L. Gunderson expanded his investigation and confirmed the theft and sale of missing tapes made by people interviewed under court order. At the time, the Omaha World-Herald newspaper became the first daily newspaper to discuss the case against it when a broadcast employee filed regular articles so the public would hear evidence the judge had ordered. This was done during radio segments of the French Connection talk show. Despite Gunderson's efforts, the entire investigation was blocked by the deliberate loss of evidence everywhere.

Boys and Girls Clubs are breeding grounds for exploitation

Boys and Girls Clubs have long been regarded as safe havens for children, providing recreational activities, mentorship, and support in communities across the globe. However, beneath the surface of these trusted institutions lies a disturbing reality: they can serve as breeding grounds for exploitation, with traffickers preying upon the trust and vulnerability of unsuspecting children. This paper delves into the complexities of how Boys and Girls Clubs, while well-intentioned, can inadvertently become targets for traffickers, and the urgent need for awareness and vigilance to protect children from exploitation within these environments.

A. Boys and Girls Clubs are often perceived as safe havens for children, offering a range of recreational activities, educational programs, and supportive services. These clubs play a vital role in providing a positive and nurturing environment where children can learn, grow, and thrive under the guidance of caring adults. However, this perception of safety can create a false sense of security, leading parents, staff, and volunteers to overlook the potential risks of exploitation lurking within these seemingly protective spaces.

A. Traffickers exploit the trust and accessibility of Boys and Girls Clubs to target vulnerable children who may lack parental supervision or guidance. By infiltrating these institutions, traffickers gain access to a pool of potential victims who may be seeking attention, validation, or a sense of belonging. Traffickers may pose as mentors, volunteers, or even fellow club members, leveraging their position of trust to groom and manipulate children into compliance. The familiarity and camaraderie fostered within Boys and Girls Clubs can make it easier for traffickers to establish relationships with their victims and maintain control over them without arousing suspicion.

A. Despite their noble mission and positive impact on communities, Boys and Girls Clubs may be ill-equipped to recognize and respond to the threat of trafficking within their midst. Parents, staff, and volunteers may be unaware of the signs and indicators of exploitation, overlooking red flags or dismissing behavior as harmless. Moreover, the stigma and taboo surrounding the issue of trafficking may deter individuals from acknowledging its presence within these environments, allowing exploitation to go undetected and unaddressed.

Boys and Girls Clubs play a vital role in supporting the healthy development and well-being of children, but they are not immune to the insidious influence of child sex trafficking. By understanding the vulnerabilities inherent within these environments and the tactics used by traffickers to exploit them, communities can work together to strengthen safeguards, raise awareness, and empower children to recognize and resist exploitation. Only through collective action and vigilance can we ensure that Boys and Girls Clubs remain true safe havens for all children, free from the scourge of exploitation.

The Boy Scouts of America (BSA) was incorporated in 1910 and chartered by the U.S. Congress in 1916. Commonly referred to as a youth development organization, the BSA aims to instill desired qualities of citizenship, national pride, moral fiber, discipline, friendship, achievements, and a strong character. "The values found in the Boy Scout Oath and the Scout Law are the foundation of scouting and are relevant for young people and their adult leaders." The Scout's code of conduct, character building, personal fitness, leadership, community involvement, ability to think on their feet, adapt to schedule changes, confront and solve problems, make thoughtful decisions, think for themselves, contribute to scout meetings, and remain optimistic are fundamental stepping stones to help shape these young men.

Child sexual abuse has been a persistent issue throughout the years, affecting families and communities. We believe that our organization is not excluded from this problem. We don't need statistics to validate the risks of abuse, even within our organization. Many parents have entrusted their child's safety, development, and growth to the Scouts, allured by the camaraderie between Scouts and Central Florida Scouting (CFC). This bond has withstood decades of excellence due to the leadership of many dedicated volunteers. However, incredible acts of goodness often overshadow a single incident that can bring down something delicious. We hope that by unveiling our truth, the CFC may initiate an open dialogue on this subject, potentially benefiting our community and the Boy Scouts of America.

Today, the Boy Scouts of America is one of our nation's iconic institutions, as prized as another presidential portrait. This organization was motivated by values ranging from superiority in leadership to duty to God. But in recent years, the Boy Scouts of America has been better known by its most unfortunate acronym, BSA. This organization is, in fact, the fabric that has consumed its thread. Decades of private negotiations failed to stitch back the moral leaf from the recent sexual predation outbreak, which is now officially described as a "Sexual Abuse Crisis." These self-inflicted challenges are, of course, not unlike the ones that the Catholic Church bore for a similarly interminable period. But today, these are the Boy Scouts of America's problems.

Seventy-eight years ago, Life magazine described the Boy Scouts of America as one of 10 educationally sound and democratic institutions that produced high-minded, fit, and healthy people. Norman Rockwell captured these young Scouts' earnest and caring lives in nearly 5,000 canvas portraits. Fast forward to 2021, the Boy Scouts of America continues to be the epitome of middle-class youth leadership development. Many celebrities have passed muster in this organization and eventually given back time and treasure. From John F. Kennedy in the civil rights era to George W. Bush, former United States presidents spilled their political plans in infomercial-quality narratives.

The myriad of allegations of sexual abuse within the Boy Scouts of America. For many of the accused perpetrators, this organization was the source of constant underage male potential victims, often called Boy Scouts. We describe and analyze the suspected predators, both the Boy Scout leaders or volunteers who were never employed by BSA and the positive role model professional Scouters who were also involved. Conceptually, we use Laurie's Risk Propensity Model - categorizing offenders by their risk associated with access to potential victims: destination offenders (the perpetrators who sought out the opportunities and spent time at the Boy Scout-sponsored programs), situational (the volunteers and leaders who hide within the legitimate program for victims), opportunistic (anyone who happens to be present and have contact with the potential victim), and ordinance (any attachment to society that gives one access to victims - this is primarily for the professional scouters or other employed scouters who had abundant access to potential boy scout victims during or after Scouting but also for those who are broadening their criminal horizons to include boys because their access to their old victim pool diminishes due to age, etc.). We draw empirical data primarily from the three thousand thirty-one Boy Scout Leader Perversion Files. Beyond a complete demographic analysis of the accused, we studied their readiness for deviance, the abuse contexts, and the heterogeneity among the accused.

In 2011, the Oregon Supreme Court upheld a punitive jury verdict against the BSA in the case of Kerry Lewis, who "was a shy, quiet 13-year-old altar boy when the Scoutmaster at his Roman Catholic church sexually abused him in 1983. He was 38 when the trial took place in 2010." Lewis claimed that neither the church nor the BSA had "any awareness of the potential for sexual abuse by adult volunteers and leaders within the organization" – despite a half-century of internal documentation suggesting otherwise, as well as testimony being offered in which the BSA's former national security director continued to maintain that it didn't "have the same level of sophistication about sexual abuse as society does today." In the years since, this "lack of understanding," as well as subsequent claims of "opportunity" for such abuse to take place, has been deflated by as many as thousands of media reports, numerous politicians, and who knows how many 'regular' citizens of this country's knowledge of benefiting from some form of Scouting.

Sexual abuse within the nation's largest scouting organization, the Boy Scouts of America (BSA), did not simply happen two decades ago or even thirty or forty years ago. It virtually predates the official organization when Baden Powell, who later established the BSA, founded the Boy Scouts of England over a century ago. In the decade since litigation has brought this cataclysmic problem of youth abuse to the BSA forefront, we are now realizing that this abhorrent conduct exudes itself from the very fabric of the 'institutions' themselves. The dangerous pretense of child safety within the organization cannot be protected within the wrapper of touting "good" intentions. It should never have taken more than a century within the U.S.-based BSA institution to protect the children it serves from the actions of pedophiles.

In 1943, Ova Miller published an article in the Journal of Educational Sociology which investigated the role of the BSA in preventing juvenile delinquency. The 912 volunteers were asked about the activities and issues in their councils. In response to the question, "Are there any members in your council who are known to be homosexuals or assaults on boys?" 111 or 12.2% of the respondents answered "Yes" to this question. Although this initial response was defined using Boolean logic rather than a false dichotomy and reported verbatim to the percentage, the lead researcher surmised only one "Yes" response was "believable." Additional research showed that despite significant firewalling attempts by the BSA, the study authors and subsequent researchers detailed massive dilemmas with the national publication's circulation and replication. In 1947, a Boy Scout in Boston wrote to Sir Winston Churchill and claimed homosexuals had infiltrated the Boston chapter while there were also threats of boycotts at the annual Boston gathering as well.

The first corroborated reports of sexual abuse within the BSA occurred in the 1920s. The BSA's estimated annual publication, Scouter (now known as Scouting), reported that "many of the worst enemies of the Boy Scout movement today were at one time members of the staff of Scoutmasters and were exposed by the movement." By the early 1930s, the Managing Secretary, Dr. James E. West, wrote to the local Scout officials regarding the "danger of fostering bad sexual habits by allowing boys to camp together." In the 1931 Scouter, he also wrote about "the emperor is stark naked, even though he wants to persuade himself that he has a nifty outfit of clothes, equal to any tailor-made raiment on the market" while standing rather than "prowl around in a masquerade robe of wolf's skin."

The Boy Scouts of America is the largest scouting organization in the world, with over 2 million members. It claims to teach community service, citizenship, and other "value-based activities." Due to the Boy Scouts' size and diversity, they are not considered part of any religious denomination and, therefore, cannot claim the privilege of the Catholic Church, as discussed in case 1.2.1. If the sexual abuse had been publicized and shown to be inherent within the Boy Scouts as it was in the Catholic Church, the Boy Scouts could have been brought down in minutes. Nevertheless, the very public, incredibly ridiculous image of the Boy Scouts organization led the 12 million former Boy Scouts now brought together in this class action lawsuit.

To make matters worse, the Boy Scouts of America actively silenced those who reported the abuse that they suffered. The organization created and maintained "ineligible volunteer" or "perversion" lists, which were secret lists of people who were accused or removed for allegations of sexual misconduct made against them and, by the pre-1970s, knowledge of committing other crimes or fraud. Additionally, the Boy Scouts actively surveyed all of its local camps for possible activities. Over the 72 years, the BSA received over 12,000 abuse reports from boys in their organization. The issue of child predators infiltrating the Boy Scouts was made even worse by the fact that incredibly few were reported to law enforcement. In the Bartholome above case, only five of the 250+ files were directly reported to law enforcement. The Boy Scouts' failure to report known abuse and its role in covering up said abuse patterns is apparent.

Sexual abuse constantly delivers devastating blows to the hurt individuals and families, but it goes beyond the survivor. The destruction also hits the people and families of the survivors due to reduced personal contact that follows persistent withdrawal from social circles. The role of the media in this regard is well explained by Pender, who states that "if an individual is no longer able to perform daily activities and therefore people are no longer in touch with one another, then it is likely that media will play the role of determining people's opinions become important; the media has also taken over 'control' over inter-individual encounters. Therefore, if such encounters no longer take place, the media's portrayal determines, in the interactions between individuals, the criteria for selecting interaction partners, interpreting the latter's opinions, and providing information about them". Abused individuals and families find it hard to control the cycle of withdrawal and alienation. I can confidently say that sexual abuse's usual plot involves networks of people who are capable of harassing and ruining the lives of severe and honest individuals.

Sexual abuse has severe consequences for the many victims, girls, and boys equally, as it negatively influences almost all intricate aspects of life. An insecure family environment, inability to cope, aggression, dependency, unruly behavior, unhappiness, mental health problems, financial obstacles, illness, and fear are some of the adverse long-term impacts that may surface instantaneously or years later. Victims have more chances of performing poorly in their education, are unable to secure jobs, and may fall victim to criminal behaviors. For the many boys under the Boy Scouts of America mentioned within the Perversion Files, wounds from sexual abuse have led to distancing close relationships with other people and also withdrawing trust in legitimate sources of leadership and fellowship "... it may be that they are the person everyone thinks of, but no one knows".

In 2019 alone, over one hundred lawsuits were filed in NYC under the Child Victims Act. In Kentucky, 4,800 former Boy Scouts took legal action to seek compensation from the BSA for the sexual abuse they endured. In most cases across the U.S., the BSA has declined to respond publicly regarding the number of lawsuits filed and the number of former Scouts involved. The problem of sexual assault was a derivative of a growing youth movement in the early 20th century. The rise of various associations and more formal groups dedicated to the service and education of boys emphasized the outdoors, individual preparedness, the ability to withstand hardship, as well as character development, citizenship, and the necessity of working with younger boys whenever possible. The father of parochial-based organizations, Ernest Temme, a Lutheran minister, was the first to mention the need for parents to know their children would be protected by a Scoutmaster, who would be trained to care for that child by the BSA. Once a child joined these promising groups of associated Scoutmasters and individual members of the BSA itself, they were placed on an informal social register, of sorts, as one of the chosen higher-order young men that society and their parents trusted in their care and development.

Hundreds and possibly thousands of former Boy Scouts, along with their families, learned for the first time over the past several months disturbing information about their local Scoutmasters, who spent weekend camping trips, nighttime meetings, and summer vacations gaining access to groups of unsuspecting boys. In fact, according to information received by our firm and other lawyers, the local leaders' unauthorized conduct has been a systemic problem throughout the fifty-year history of the Boy Scouts of America. It is not confined to any particular geographic, ethnic, or income group. The revelation of the Boy Scouts of America's failure over several decades resulted in thousands of lawsuits filed nationwide. National, state, and local media articles report the extent of the stories with no shortage of plaintiffs willing to step forward. The abuse affected Scouts in a variety of ways – some would act out, some turned to drugs or alcohol, while others suffered a crisis of faith. Some questioned their sexuality. Many would suffer psychological trauma for the rest of their lives. The abuse was a betrayal on the most fundamental level – one's very own Scoutmasters caused the destruction.

According to reports, once Mr. Ralph Dickerson, the BSA's national director, was informed of the survey results, he told those conducting the inquiry to stop. No one looked at what the reports contained, nor did a statistical analysis of what was reported.

As a result of this inquiry, 1,622 individuals were determined to have been removed from Scouting through 1971, and those files were maintained and put into storage to prevent these individuals from returning to Scouting. These documents contained informal descriptions, letters, reports, and other correspondence related to the individuals removed from positions. However, these records often contained information that the BSA determined did not rise to the levels of criminal involvement or was dismissed at a level where law enforcement agencies were not involved.

After an investigation, Seehausen's attorney discovered that there were 17 registered sex offenders in Oregon who, at one time, had been associated with Scouting. This report, along with the records requested during the litigation, highlighted a significant issue regarding the "confidential files" used by the BSA to keep track of individuals who were removed from Scouting positions when it was deemed to be for reasons of misconduct. These files had existed since the 1920s, yet the BSA had determined that these were not to be released when they conducted a national inquiry in the 1970s.

In 2007, the Oregon Supreme Court issued a decision for the three Seehausen brothers who brought suit against the Boy Scouts of America. This case involved several men who had been identified as registered sex offenders and had had legal contact with the plaintiffs. The boys had been sexually molested before 1987 by one of their troop leaders and filed suit in 2002.

I remember being a boy, I was despondent and tearful on Father's Day, but I didn't know why. I asked my mother what was wrong with me. She said she didn't understand why I was like that and suggested we talk to a counselor. I didn't understand then why I didn't feel so bad on Mother's Day. I felt incredibly close to my mom, more so than usual, on that day and the day before and after. A few years ago, shortly after my sleepless nights began, when my screaming started again, I remembered that I had been sexually abused as a child, and I connected it to why I felt such disdain on Father's Day. I was molested and raped by a man who had a mustache, looked somewhat like my father, and smelled of cigarettes and liquor. The Boy Scouts had trained and presented him as a moral and upstanding citizen. What I also suddenly remembered is that when I realized most recently that this man had sexually abused me, I went to my mother and asked her if she felt that there had been "anything special" about me when I was young, particularly when I was, say around 11 or 12 years of age. She said I had always been special but became suspicious and asked me why. I couldn't tell her what had happened. For years, she confided in me that she desperately tried to figure out what "special" meant but that I had suddenly clammed up and refused to discuss something else I had surfaced. She frequently expressed to me the guilt she felt as a mother for failing to understand why I was sad and also the sense of guilt she felt for the uncertainty that overwhelmed her at the time I came to her with sadness. I could never discuss with her how horrible I felt or tell her why. I was silent then, just as I am now, and I promised her when I put her on the ground that I would never let anyone know what had happened to me. Even now, I do not doubt that his secret molestation of me contributed to my father's self-abuse with alcohol and his eventual death from cancer. I've partially cracked open the vault and have told a few close friends who never would have guessed the extent of the inner hell that I suffer. I am writing this statement because Pandora's Box opened slightly with the lawsuit against the Boy Scouts of America, and the tremendous stress I've been experiencing the past few years is causing me to disassociate further, more than usual.

These are the words that I've never spoken but which I hope will somehow help heal me.

In 2010, Kerry Lewis was awarded nearly $20 million in compensatory and punitive damages - a remarkable case, as it was the first decision against the Boy Scouts of America from a jury trial. The extensive amount of money awarded to Kerry was partially because the Boy Scouts of America failed to provide the proper documentation during the investigation and then failed to implement the requested changes. In 2011, the highest award until that point was presented for the sexual abuse he suffered. It was 18.5 million dollars and awarded to a young man, who, at the time known as "Doe 1," accused a Santa Barbara scoutmaster of abusing him. These two cases are significant. They showed the Boy Scouts of America that, unfortunately, no good could ever come from concealing documents or ignoring survivors. "It's amazing that countless attempts, emails, phone calls, and formal letters did not budge the BSA. These were met with nothing but sheer intimidation and similar tactics showing extreme disregard for the families' well-being," Lewis says. To fully comprehend the corruption and negligence present in the organization, one must fully understand the amount of shame that these boys felt at the time the Boy Scouts rapes occurred. These were examples of how "silent" he thought he had to be following the assault:

Upon entering the 2,500 on-field records obtained from the Supreme Court of Texas into a database of sexual offenses, it became apparent that 1 in 6 of the supervisory leaders in the state of Texas have been accused of practicing sexual abuse with a victim or victims. On this basis alone, in 2001, the Los Angeles Times' series of exposes (and those of the Philadelphia Inquirer, Canadian Broadcasting Corporation, and BBC) may have illustrated the fact that widespread sexual misconduct has been a characteristic of the Boy Scouts of America since its inception in 1910. These studies stand as the only longitudinal monitoring of sexual abuse on children or by children anywhere in the world. This metric has persisted since 1992 and is next to unchanged, except for a brief episode in 2001 and the P.A. prosecution stalls prompted by the public coverage of the abusive patterns shown within the BSA. The most recent (actual year 2019) calculation indicates that 90,726 and 90,174 supervisory "leaders" have not been accused of a sexual offense over the past 109 years. Indicate that 1 in 6 (17.13%) of these leaders have been registered as abusers since the BSA's creation. In direct opposition to the celestial existence of its universally recognized moral rectitude, the accumulation of contradictory data from various BSA sources throughout different legal cases supports that risk within this youth developmental organization has deteriorated over time as experienced membership has increased.

The pervasiveness of sexual abuse within the Boy Scouts of America has been highlighted within various media outlets throughout the years. In 1991, the Los Angeles Times and Investigative Reporters and Editors released data indicating that the BSA had screened out applicants for volunteer positions and subjected successful applicants to checks to ascertain whether they had previously identified offenders. As these checks had uncovered potentially disqualifying criminal records, the BSA also performed more thorough investigations, including public record checks, child abuse registry checks, and checks of the "references" that candidates provided on their applications. Combining their data with that from the BSA and a separate public Senate Report, the L.A. Times reported clustering the sexual behavior of boys in general, leaders registered as offender sex abuse as a consequence of youthful male victims, leading in 2001 to the publication of a study estimating that the BSA had destroyed some records and redacted all others of many young victims of unspecified unwanted incidents during the preceding 23 years. The 2001 study triggered widespread public coverage of the BSA's prolonged suppression of sexually suggestive records. It caused the organization finally to release some of the information that it had obtained in the Senate hearing on sexual abuse of children in the USA. A summary of the public comments and testimonies in the meeting's official record referred to the "tentacles of a mammoth criminal syndicate virtually ran (sic) the Boy Scouts." The public scandal that erupted at the time led to associated litigations, many of these involving former scouts who have been seeking damages for childhood abuse.

The Boy Scouts have made a series of internal reforms to combat the pervasive issue of sexual abuse among its members. These modifications can be traced back to the Warren and Terry studies. In 2009, the Boy Scouts initiated the comprehensive Youth Protection Program (YPP), which called for:

+ Criminal background checks
+ Youth protection training
+ A two-deep policy
+ Mandatory reporting of suspected abuse to child protective services
+ An extensive list of prohibited behaviors
+ An age-based supervision guideline

The training was made available online to all members of Scouting. Furthermore, the Boy Scouts pledged to cooperate in the future with all law enforcement agencies in sex abuse investigations. As of 2018, their website notes that 5.2 million leaders and youth members are trained in Youth Protection annually. One concrete result of this renewed vigilance has been the dramatic increase in the number of adult volunteers removed on suspicion of inappropriate contact with youth. In 2009, 392 adults were tagged as sexual predators; this number tripled by 2013. During this time, that figure peaked at 1038.

It was not until 2005 that the nation began to grapple with the scale of sexual abuse within the Boy Scouts of America. In response to the 2005 civil litigation, the Boys Scouts began a Review and Response Program, which culminated in two academic studies under the leadership of Janet Warren and Karen Terry. The first study, published in 2010, estimated that between 1948 and 2005, approximately 5,000 unique adults were reported by the Scouts to authorities for sexually abusing youth within their leadership. The second study unearthed over 12,200 suspected victims who reported abuse at the hands of these adults. Despite the release of this shocking report, also in 2012, the Boy Scouts had still neglected to release the nearly 2,000 additional files associated with these suspected abusers, which Koss's 2012 PEW report had indicated were being hidden in internal BSA archives.

Other actions the BSA took during the 1985 screening standard implementation involved offering video and printed resources to 2900 districts regarding prevention and guidance in identifying potential abusers. To ensure underage boys reporting acts of abuse had access to someone to share with, in 1987, over 15,000 troop leaders attended six specialized training courses. Requested focuses for these included the unique aspects involved in boys' abuse experiences and the potential impact that their efforts towards unity, neutrality, and approachability would have on an abused or potentially abused boy, allowing him the space to create a transformative dialogue with someone he trusted. In addition, BSA also disseminated a plethora of printed resources to educate and inform boys and adult volunteers about the issues involved. Formalized in reaction to lawsuit judgments in 1980 and 1992, it was applied in 100 local councils, districts, and thousands of Boy Scout troops.

For the BSA, attempts to prevent sexual abuse spanned the last seven decades. Document review revealed that adjustments to its policies and procedures were carefully crafted by two of its many department instructors or commissioned study groups. Beginning with efforts to discourage sex with camp workers, in 1970, the BSA established procedures for receiving and responding to accusations of boy-on-boy abuse. In contrast, staff members accused of abusing boys were referred to law enforcement. Protocols for educating boys, leaders, and professionals were developed by the recommendations of two hired clinical psychologists and, later, a Boy Scout Division's Mental Health and Camping Task Force.

The Betrayal of Trust and Sanctuary by Churches

Churches hold a revered place in society as sanctuaries of worship and community, providing congregants solace, guidance, and spiritual nourishment. However, this sanctity can be shattered by the insidious presence of child sex trafficking, as traffickers exploit the trust and vulnerability of both children and their families within these hallowed spaces. This section delves into the unsettling reality of how churches, symbols of faith and sanctuary, can become arenas of exploitation and the profound betrayal of trust and faith that ensues.

Churches, revered as sanctuaries of solace and spiritual nourishment, are meant to be places of refuge and trust. However, the reality is starkly different as traffickers exploit the vulnerability and accessibility of these sacred spaces to prey upon innocent children. This paper delves into the insidious phenomenon of child exploitation within churches, exploring the dynamics of trust, betrayal, and the urgent need for vigilance and accountability.

Churches hold a sacred place in the hearts of worshippers, serving as havens where individuals seek guidance, community, and divine protection. Within these hallowed walls, congregants find solace from life's challenges and cultivate bonds of fellowship and faith. The inherent sanctity of churches fosters a sense of trust and security among worshippers, who view these spaces as bastions of spiritual nourishment and divine intervention.

Unfortunately, the sanctity of churches also makes them vulnerable targets for traffickers seeking to exploit the trust and faith of worshippers. Traffickers infiltrate congregations, posing as trusted members of the faith community, to gain access to vulnerable children. Under the guise of faith and goodwill, they manipulate and groom children, luring them into situations of exploitation and abuse under the cloak of religious legitimacy. The accessibility and perceived safety of churches make them ideal hunting grounds for traffickers seeking to prey upon the innocence of children.

The exploitation of children within the confines of a church represents a profound betrayal of faith and a violation of sacred trust. Congregants entrust their spiritual well-being and that of their children to the care of religious leaders and community members, only to have that trust exploited for nefarious purposes. The desecration of a space meant for worship and reverence with acts of exploitation and abuse shatters the very foundation of faith and undermines the moral authority of religious institutions.

The exploitation of children within churches is a devastating betrayal of trust and faith, striking at the heart of our collective values and beliefs. To combat this insidious phenomenon, we must acknowledge the vulnerabilities inherent within religious communities and the tactics used by traffickers to exploit them. Strengthening safeguards, raising awareness, and fostering a culture of vigilance and accountability within our faith institutions are imperative steps toward upholding the sanctity of our faith and ensuring the safety and well-being of all children within our communities. Only by confronting the uncomfortable reality of exploitation within sacred spaces can we protect the innocence and preserve the integrity of our faith traditions.

As we write this one of the SRA'S and cases of abuse, the Dark Reality Behind the Hosanna Church Sex Abuse Scandal In a harrowing tale reminiscent of a dark crime drama, the Hosanna Church in Ponchatoula, Louisiana, once a vibrant center of faith and community, descended into the depths of horror and depravity. What began as a flourishing evangelical institution, with thousands of devoted members and a commitment to educational initiatives, metamorphosed into a nightmarish saga of abuse and trauma that would haunt the town for years to come. The Hosanna Church, once teeming with life and vibrant worship, witnessed a stark decline in its congregation, plunging from a vibrant community of 1,000 members to a mere handful of reclusive individuals. The catalyst for this downfall was a ferocious falling-out between the pastor's son and successor, Louis Lamonica Jr., and his family, a rift that tore at the church's fabric and left it fractured and vulnerable. Within the shadows of the Hosanna Church, a sinister cult took root, its tendrils spreading insidiously through the once-hallowed halls. Reports surfaced of devil worship and occult rituals, with members cloaked in black robes and engaging in unspeakable acts of sexual abuse against innocent children. The cult's activities, shrouded in darkness and secrecy, were fueled by a disturbing blend of power and perversion. In a chilling parallel to the narrative of "True Detective," individuals entrusted with positions of authority within the church were implicated in grotesque crimes. Louis Lamonica Jr., the pastor's son and successor, along with a 24-year-old sheriff's deputy, stood accused of participating in the abuse ring. Shockingly, the former pastor himself confessed to heinous acts of abuse against numerous children, including his sons, perpetuating a cycle of depravity and trauma. The revelation of such appalling crimes sent shockwaves through the tight-knit community of Ponchatoula, leaving residents reeling in disbelief and horror. The accusations of occult practices, including devil worship and sacrificial rituals, added a layer of terror, casting a pall of fear and suspicion over the town. The mysteries surrounding the cult's activities left scars that would linger long after the church's doors closed for the final time. Law enforcement officials relentlessly pursued truth and accountability, determined to bring the perpetrators to justice. Witnesses bravely came forward, providing crucial testimony that shed light on the dark underbelly of the Hosanna Church. Despite the cult's efforts to evade detection, authorities remained steadfast in their quest for justice, uncovering the extent of the atrocities committed within the church's walls.

As legal proceedings unfolded and arrests were made, the once-hallowed grounds of the Hosanna Church stood as a chilling testament to the evils that lurked within. The church's closure marked the end of an era, leaving behind a legacy of horror and betrayal that would haunt the town for generations to come. Yet, amid the darkness, there remained a glimmer of hope for redemption and healing as the community rallied together to confront the demons of its past.

The Hosanna Church sex abuse scandal stands as a stark reminder of the fragility of faith and the capacity for human depravity. It is a cautionary tale against the dangers of unchecked power and the insidious influence of darkness. As the community grapples with the scandal's aftermath, the victims may find solace and justice, and the memory of their suffering catalyzes change and renewal in pursuing a brighter, safer future.

Avoiding Child Trafficking Riskier sex trafficking

Shielding Innocence Strategies for Combating Child Recruitment and Exploitation Increases Children's Vulnerability to Sex Trafficking In today's world, the safety and well-being of children are threatened by the insidious tactics of traffickers and exploiters. To address this urgent issue, we must implement comprehensive strategies that raise awareness, strengthen safeguarding measures, and empower children to protect themselves. This book delves into the details of these strategies, providing practical insights and actionable steps to combat recruitment and exploitation effectively.

In this chapter, we explore the importance of education and awareness campaigns in combating child trafficking and exploitation. By shedding light on the tactics used by traffickers and the subtle signs of recruitment, we empower parents, caregivers, and community members to be vigilant guardians of children's safety. Through informative workshops, targeted outreach programs, and engaging media campaigns, we equip individuals with the knowledge they need to recognize and respond to potential threats.

Here, we delve into the critical role of institutions in protecting children from exploitation. We examine the necessity of robust safeguarding policies and procedures in schools, childcare facilities, religious institutions, and other community organizations. By implementing stringent background checks, strict access control measures, and comprehensive training for staff, institutions can create safe environments where children are shielded from harm and traffickers are deterred from gaining access.

In this chapter, we highlight the power of education in empowering children to safeguard themselves against exploitation. We discuss the importance of providing age-appropriate lessons on personal safety, boundaries, and healthy relationships in schools and communities. Through interactive workshops, role-playing activities, and open dialogues, we encourage children to develop assertiveness, critical thinking skills, and confidence in their ability to recognize and resist exploitation. By empowering children with knowledge and agency, we fortify them against the tactics of traffickers and empower them to assert their rights and protect their well-being.

Child sex trafficking is a harrowing reality that thrives on the vulnerability of its victims, regardless of their background or circumstances. This paper delves into the disturbing truth that withdrawn, isolated children, or those with strained parental relationships, are particularly susceptible to the horrors of trafficking. Furthermore, it examines the tragic consequences faced by these victims, whose average age ranges from 12 to 15 years, and whose lives are tragically cut short by abuse, drug overdoses, or suicide.

Traffickers prey on children who exhibit withdrawn or isolated behavior, exploiting their vulnerability and lack of robust social support networks. These children, devoid of a sense of belonging, become easy targets for traffickers who manipulate their isolation to trap them in exploitation.

Children who lack close friendships or social connections are prime targets for traffickers, who capitalize on their loneliness and yearning for acceptance. Exploiting their desire for companionship, traffickers lure these children into the darkness of trafficking with false promises of belonging and understanding.

Children experiencing conflict or tension in their relationships with parents are highly susceptible to exploitation. Seeking validation and support outside the familial sphere, they become vulnerable to the deceitful allure of traffickers offering solace and empathy. In their quest for understanding, these children fall prey to exploitation.

We have to work to ensure that well-trained, qualified security forces observe and respect human rights. Promote ways to end the practice that leads to violence and destruction. These provide young people with meaningful educational, economic, and civic opportunities for sustainable peace and development in places with conflict. We prevent the recruitment and use of children as soldiers when young people begin to perceive the hopelessness of violent solutions to problems and the value of not promoting peace, development, and respect for human rights.

It is better in the long run to take steps to prevent recruitment, including detention, than to wait until the child has been formally recruited into an irregular force, which is a significant challenge. There are no easy answers to preventing the recruitment of child soldiers, but a range of strategies are available that can help put an end to this abuse of children. These strategies must be developed at national and international levels and through governmental cooperation with civil society organizations. Most of the strategies are based on international law concerning the rights of children and, of course, principles. In every society, only the full implementation of these rights and practices can protect children from armed conflict.

Another concern addressed by child recruitment advocacy is the scope of regional regulations that attempt to govern Sierra Leone-specific issues. This critique of the non-sequitur analysis shows why multilateral and regional instruments and bodies will fail to change child recruitment in West Africa. These laws, documentation, and partnerships are concluded because persons of particular prestige and power mostly design these multilateral and regional agreements with the intention of guesstimating what discrete countries require and without respect for beneficial stakeholders. This non sequitur analysis is compounded by opportunities to provide censure and rebuke for the inadequacy of a given country's recruitment attempt. Further, the observer states that if the regional or multilateral agreements do not contribute to a specific country addressing a particular problem, then peripheral entities think that such movement is not needed in their country.

Ensuring that public and private sector institutional structures are in place to provide a protective framework for children is the first critical step to original social and economic violence and exploitation of children. This section itemizes national and regional laws that aim to discharge that mandate. A scholarly review of regional and national laws addressing child recruitment specifically argues that the roles of various stakeholders tackling child recruitment are more unclear and uncoordinated than clear and coordinated. When European Union, United Nations, and African Union officials and programs interfere with national or regional level efforts to combat child recruitment, the result is multidimensional dysfunction, pictured by the uneven distillation of donor funds, preventing North-South research collaboration between Africa and the West, and local level avoiding both child and improper de facto peace jurisdiction as the conundrum of the community-based truth. Measures that should be in place to stop child recruitment include rules that are discerning of age, proportional advancement systems, age-appropriate measures, and skill levels that connect with current life activities.

To do this, there are three strategic pillars to the education response. First, there is a need to analyze, use, develop, and reflect on data about why different individuals enter, stay in, or leave—during or after school—armed forces and groups. There is a need to develop an understanding of the key factors associated with entry, attrition, and sustained engagement in these forces and groups. It is important to gather evidence about the educational and socioeconomic status of the families of children who are targeted or recruited by terrorist organizations and the paths they follow. It is also important to take into account durable solutions, including reintegration into communities and learning opportunities available to children who have gone through rehabilitation centers. It is unnecessary to use a variety of data gathering methods, including household surveys, mainly in countries with settings of conflict, variable poverty, and children recruited into armed conflict; studies that use rapid mobile survey approaches in refugee and internally displaced communities, and studies combined with existing population-based surveys in settings with communities receiving reintegration support. For instance, a situation of armed conflict or internally displaced people is against a specific number of survey methods. While family or community members could hold perspectives on a child's stay in forces or armed groups, other up to 60 young adult forces or groups and politicians or representatives from the forces who may also have the perspective of young persons may need to be integrated to enter the group and agree to participate in a survey.

Efforts to prevent child recruitment can be made at the local level by providing children with access to rehabilitative alternative educational and social reintegration programs. The impacts of conflict have made child welfare and education especially important, as these services can increase a child's future employment prospects and reduce his or her vulnerability to future exploitation of any nature. Furthermore, alternative educational programs can help to restore the safety of former child soldiers. The greatest protection for a child is his or her ability, at any place, to foster a relationship with knowledgeable adults; preventing child recruitment and rehabilitating children are crucial societal investments to raise healthy prospective adults who can help in the development of the country. These programs can be relevant for all children affected by a crisis, and therefore, the reduction of risk for all children must be the primary objective. The second overarching goal of the education response to child recruitment is to ensure that quality educational opportunities are available to these children through formal and non-formal education programming.

The return and reintegration programs, through their focus on rabbits, have provided an income generation component, which often directly benefits the returning trafficked women. A project in one rural district worked to prevent childhood vulnerabilities, which it identified as the main problems facing children. The way it prevented child vulnerability was to provide income generation training and support to local women, who were then able to provide for the health and education needs of their own and other local families, as well as form youth discussion groups to prevent other childhood exploitation. This single project successfully addressed multiple issues, including preventing child vulnerability, by benefiting women.

The return and reintegration programs in Nepal for trafficked men, women, and children have included or assisted in developing vocational and income generation initiatives, particularly for women. Fewer options have been available to prevent re-trafficking. However, some initiatives have provided income generation support without providing vocational skills, which has resulted in those benefiting from the project expanding their businesses or finding labor opportunities within their communities. This has been in the context of larger return programs involving men and women rather than those specific to children.

As soon as children are newly enrolled in an armed group, the first requirement is to take care of their basic needs for food, shelter, medical care, and access to external assistance. Here, the aim is to provide the children with the support and attention they need during a period of acute emotional stress. However, the further reintegration process has the primary goal of enabling the girls and boys who have fought for the ideological or other reasons of an armed conflict to voluntarily and non-authoritatively return to the care of their parents – particularly difficult in the case of the "forgotten" children, who sometimes have not seen a lot of their families for a very long time. A gradual reintegration process, which, in a broader sense, considers the school and vocational training of the young people as well as the trauma-oriented care measures, belongs to the adolescents, supports this goal. These may overlap; very generally, young people usually move from one phase to the next if they have found a certain degree of psychological stability that allows them to participate reasonably in these measures.

This section focuses on the suffering of children and adolescents once they have left an armed group and need psychosocial help. This is essential as psychological trauma is widespread and often overlooked, undermining adolescents' reintegration and rehabilitation processes. For most former child and youth soldiers, life in the group has been synonymous with physical and emotional abuse, and children often have to take on roles that go far beyond their personal resistance and psychological limits. Against the background of their traumatic experiences, questions about children and whether they want to or can return can be difficult to answer. Trust, honesty, and consideration for the children and young people must be the focus of the work.

Child sex trafficking thrives on the vulnerability of its victims, exploiting their emotional needs and strained relationships. By acknowledging these vulnerabilities and implementing targeted interventions, we can work towards protecting children from falling victim to this heinous crime. It is imperative that we strengthen support networks, promote healthy relationships, and empower children to recognize and resist the tactics of traffickers. Only through concerted efforts can we create a safer environment for our children, shielding them from exploitation and ensuring their well-being and dignity and our exploration of strategies to combat recruitment and exploitation of children, we recognize the collective responsibility we bear to safeguard the innocence and dignity of our youngest members. By heightening awareness, strengthening safeguarding measures, and empowering children, we can build a resilient barrier against the scourge of child trafficking and exploitation. Together, let us stand as vigilant defenders of childhood, ensuring that every child is afforded the opportunity to grow and thrive in safety and security.

Addressing Vulnerability in Trafficking Victims' Mental Impact

The Tragic Fate of Victims' Average Age Victims of child sex trafficking are generally aged 12 to 15, emphasizing teenagers' susceptibility to exploitation. Shortened life expectancy victims of trafficking endure severe physical and psychological suffering, resulting in a tragically short life expectancy. Causes Of Premature Death Victims may suffer from maltreatment, drug overdoses, or suicide as a consequence of the anguish imposed on them by traffickers.

When GEMS (Girls Educational and Mentoring Services) was founded in 1998, the average age of prostitution entry was 14 years old. Recent data suggests an average age of 12 years. In 2017, about 10% of sex trafficking survivors were in their 50s-60s at the entrance, while 1100-1300 new survivors were assisted by GEMS each year. GEMS visits schools and communities to discuss vulnerabilities to sex trafficking. Surveys of young people we spoke with indicated they would rather be with a peer running a life they see as independent and exciting due in part to age, maturity, and legal career opportunities. Impact requires the sharing to come from people their age, or a few years older, who have loved and lost, remain, or perhaps only recently survived the encounters with severe crises. A changing team of translators educated villages, pointing out where village children might go when the families did not think they were watching. Social media reports of successful life changes of some survivors we met surprised us by spreading from the remote villages to some of the survivors we met. An indigo shawl indicates freedom understood and admired, presenting visual and emotional testimony in village family locations by successful survivors they had neither seen in person nor heard about in student sessions.

With the terms victims and sex trafficking readily identified and understood by the general public, the average age of both prostitution and sex trafficking is a surprise. Calculations allow for easy transfer to the U.S. from the study location. The average age for entry into prostitution in Madurai, India, and thus sex trafficking into the U.S., continues to decrease. We must use well-vetted survivor voices to address national and worldwide vulnerability. Education on early intervention, awareness, prevention tactics, community-based support, and well-chosen care approaches must work together to create the possibility for all to seek and sustain a life disconnected from harm.

Victims of child sex trafficking: The tragic fate of their average age. Psychological impact: Addressing vulnerability and trauma.

In general, both extensive studies review the most recent recommendations on trauma recovery approaches, which will have long-term success if effectively implemented. However, many TIC core components may unintentionally contribute to ongoing reactive considerations. A brief review of care/TIC literature highlights the importance of empowering TIC to develop proactive and meaningful responses to prevent ongoing complex trauma. By combining individual, family, community, and political perspectives, the components of trauma care address the potential need by empowering individuals to recognize the need for preventive interventions. In essence, training children requires TIC to be proud of their capacity. However, the conduct of trauma does not include how to approach children and adolescents who do not want help. These effects notice how training can lead to success and are accompanied by volunteers in the efforts of small children.

Providing care to victims of child sex trafficking or adolescent relationships involves complex and often challenging strategies. Practitioners need to understand how to meet these children's needs and help them cope with lifelong challenges, especially those in impossible situations. Children's current and quality service improvement models and their implementation should highlight the domains of the proposed approach. It shows essential connections between domains that need to connect to effectively support people with psychological training and a need for a strategic and long-term visionary approach to integrating meaningful interventions over a lifetime.

The exploitation and abuse endured by trafficking victims have devastating consequences for their physical, emotional, and psychological well-being. Children subjected to trafficking suffer immense trauma and are robbed of their innocence, leaving scars that may last a lifetime.

Child sex trafficking undermines the fabric of society by perpetuating cycles of violence, trauma, and exploitation. The prevalence of trafficking erodes trust in institutions, disrupts communities, and perpetuates social inequalities, posing a significant threat to societal cohesion and well-being.

The research underscores the urgent need for action to address the crisis of child sex trafficking. Every moment counts in protecting vulnerable children from harm, and failure to act swiftly only exacerbates their suffering.

Proactive measures, such as education, awareness campaigns, and early intervention programs, are essential to prevent children from falling prey to traffickers. By equipping communities with knowledge and resources, we can empower them to identify and intervene in cases of trafficking before harm occurs.

Comprehensive victim support services, including counseling, shelter, and legal assistance, are critical in providing survivors with the care and resources they need to rebuild their lives. Investing in robust support systems is essential to ensure survivors receive the help and support they deserve.

Holding traffickers accountable through robust law enforcement efforts and legal prosecution is essential to deter future crimes and deliver justice for victims. By strengthening legal frameworks and enhancing collaboration between law enforcement agencies, we can disrupt trafficking networks and bring perpetrators to justice.

Addressing child sex trafficking requires collaboration and

coordination among government agencies, law enforcement, NGOs, civil society organizations, and communities. By working together, stakeholders can pool resources, share expertise, and implement comprehensive strategies to combat trafficking effectively.

Global cooperation is essential in combating cross-border trafficking networks and ensuring that traffickers are brought to justice regardless of jurisdiction. By fostering collaboration between countries and sharing intelligence and best practices, we can disrupt trafficking routes and dismantle global criminal networks.

The U.S. child welfare system has been overwhelmed with children in out-of-home placements. Many children under the care of child welfare agencies move across states and even nationally.

Frequently, documentation of children, mainly their foster status, is not readily accessible when law enforcement encounters children who are classified as "missing." Reforms are needed to create a cohesive technological structure that allows for the seamless transfer of information, encryption, and privacy of children who have come in contact with the child welfare system. This collaborative system to track potential victims nationwide would be of immeasurable help.

Additionally, child welfare leaders and systems need to acknowledge the irrefutable connection between their struggling efforts and runaway children's vulnerability. More importantly, collaborative strategies between child welfare and other sectors, such as mental health and education systems, need to be in place to adequately support children who have come in contact with the child welfare system, particularly children who were placed in out-of-home care but are at risk for running away. Moreover, optimized awareness, prevention, and intervention, including exploitation prevention training for professionals and foster parents who are connected with children living in foster care, can better address their unique vulnerabilities.

There are several paths forward in systematically addressing child sex trafficking and ensuring that sufficient prevention, identification, and intervention are universally achievable. It is important to note that no single strategy is enough to confront the challenges of human trafficking. Community-based strategies and responses must be rooted in culturally inclusive and responsive approaches incorporating survivors' voices. The lived and learned experiences of survivors are vital for understanding human trafficking's multifaceted nature. These voices also underscore the importance of locally targeted and responsive strategies and programs in prevention and addressing the needs of survivors. However, child sex trafficking challenges are in intersectional form with social systems shaped in every sector.

Parent education is also critical. C-SAY has participated in public workshops at Nevada schools. The workshops featured at C-SAY reached over two thousand individuals associated with law enforcement, prosecuting attorneys, school teachers, surrogates for foster children, athletic coaches, parents, and children. Community awareness encourages the community to speak out if something seems awry in a hotel or with children who may be suicidal or show up with expensive gifts. A tremendous lack of understanding and practical knowledge exists when exhibiting grooming behaviors. Sexual abuse can happen in a home with children-related stepparents and other household members, in schools, respite care, daycare, and in homeless situations. This suggests that abuse and trafficking can affect any child. Just being a child makes them vulnerable and at-risk, not to mention children of pedestrians who were killed or pedestrians killed in Nevada, homeless children. A building that is likely a sex trafficking location was found in an area that contains sexually related businesses. The business model includes a rewards card given to a customer following the pay to the business operators. An individual can then bring the child to a hotel for immediate sale. The rewards system is free to each adult brought to the hotel, which benefits themselves and the child.

Additionally, prevention and awareness programs are critical. When a child runs away or becomes homeless and is "adopted" by what appears to be a "caring" person or persons, they are often initially lured into an apartment or hotel room with a warm meal and friendly adults who seem to care. Youth are vulnerable and are quickly manipulated by receiving attention and affection from those grooming them into becoming a sex trafficking victim. By presenting as C-SAY, an organization that cares about the welfare of Nevada's missing and exploited children, it becomes much easier to engage in conversations with youth who are otherwise taught not to speak to strangers. Often, adults choose not to get involved in discussions about this unsavory crime because they think that the children's parents must be wrong if their children are getting involved in sex trafficking. Raising heightened community awareness through education and understanding that the manipulators are seasoned experts in deceit assists in propelling an ongoing campaign in our schools, extracurricular activities, and youth organizations.

4.2.7 The Criminal Justice Response to CS/CMC and Policy and Practice in CS/CMC Investigation/Prosecution. Criminal domestic violence experts agree that the criminal justice response to CS/CMC can be a reliable indicator of a criminal's perception of what is or is not accepted in society. In December 2016, the Federal Government of Nigeria (Federal Ministry of Women and Social Development Affairs) adopted the official protocol for identifying the vulnerable. It exploited children in the process system in the Central Zone to combat sexual abuse. The system is the direct outcome of the "Post Test" research on the possibility of identifying and supporting child victims of trafficking under the "Post Test Health Protocol," which was the interest's reaction and available feedback. Other key partners also include UNICEF, the European Union, and UNAIDS. This process produced necessary feedback, resulting in several review meetings, including implementing partners at various levels and federal and state-wide participants to create agreements and eliminate potential conflicts between the different service providers. Meetings were scheduled multiple times and locations so all participants shared outlines and appropriate implementation plans, including accepting revisions that all partners could assess.

The Nigerian legal system has put pertinent laws to protect children from various forms of exploitation and abuse. The new Child Rights Act 2003 is one of the child-preventing laws to promote, preserve, and safeguard children's rights, according to the United Nations, which ratified it in 1989. According to the US TIP Report, "Nigeria is a source, transit, and destination country for women and children subjected to forced labor and sex trafficking." The VAPP Act 2015 and Child Right Act 2003 provide rape and defilement laws without "table age." The charge statutes for rape (Section 218-221 of the Criminal Code) now state that the age should be 14 years instead of imposing punishment or life imprisonment for rape and defilement in any Nigerian passport 18 years. Also, long-term imprisonment or clemency could be transferred to a minor age (14). However, Section 25 of the VAPP Act 2015 on Defilement and Penetration (3-5 Years) is only imprisonment.

Title 4. Measures Taken in Nigeria to Address CSEC (4.2) Legal and Law Enforcement Measures. This can be divided into the following subheadings: The Criminal Justice Response to CS/CVMC and Policy and Practice in CS/CVMC Investigation/Prosecution.

Healing and decompressing are more easily accomplished in positive settings, which could also prove to be alternatives to recidivism, known to be especially strong in our under-represented communities. Meaningful connections, lifestyle accommodations, and encouragement can challenge self-destructive behaviors, increase self-confidence, and culturally acclimate those in need. Victims should receive comprehensive case management, including assistance accessing housing, employment, education, mental and physical health care, and legal advocacy, considering the victim's maturity, understanding, and mental health needs. Transitional housing for adults and housing and comprehensive services for minors should provide safe, secure, trauma-informed, and culturally appropriate environments. Family engagement may be necessary to support and guide youth to a safe, permanent living situation where they receive proper supervision and guidance.

Lack of specialized care, resources, and government funding compromise what communities and service organizations can provide for survivors, who often face unforeseen challenges such as coming to terms with having been trafficked, addiction, mental health issues, and isolation that stymie recovery. Decompressing in an environment supporting long-term recovery can help victims to recidivate into the hands of their trafficker or another trauma-bonded situation.

Members of the domestic sex trafficking epidemic are not criminals but rather victims forced into acts against their will and are groomed at an early age by their traffickers targeting their vulnerabilities, i.e., LGBTQ, other marginalized or foster system youth, access to mentors that may have had similar experiences and would be willing to offer one-on-one coaching or coordinate trafficked youth-specific groups could provide positive alternatives.

The urgency of action in addressing the crisis of child sex trafficking cannot be overstated. It is incumbent upon governments, organizations, and individuals to take decisive steps to protect vulnerable children, prosecute traffickers, and prevent further harm. By working together with urgency, determination, and compassion, we can combat child sex trafficking and create a safer and more just world for all.

Process Church and Conspiracies

The Process Church of the Final Judgment, often referred to as the Process Church, emerged in the late 1960s as a controversial cult with origins in Scientology. Known for their ambiguous ideology and provocative imagery, such as their distinctive logo featuring a man, woman, child, and goat, the Process Church garnered attention for their alleged brainwashing techniques and rumored connections to organized crime and political conspiracy. Their association with pop culture figures like the Rolling Stones and the Manson family further fueled their image as purveyors of the darker side of the sixties counterculture. Despite disbanding in 1974, the legacy of the Process Church endures through smaller, lesser-known sects that emerged in its wake.

The Process Church of the Final Judgment, founded by ex-Scientology members, originated in the UK before expanding to the USA in the late 1960s. Initially resembling a self-help group, it evolved into a controversial cult known for its Christian-inspired beliefs and communal living arrangements. Despite being linked to conspiracy theories and infamous individuals like Charles Manson, the group's actual nature was far from the sensationalized portrayals. It attracted members through street recruiting and rituals aimed at mutual support and evangelical outreach. With its peak membership reaching up to 99 individuals, the Process Church disbanded in 1974, with some co-founders maintaining a smaller group for a few more years. However, misconceptions about the group's activities and affiliations persist due to its association with deviant individuals and sensationalized media coverage.

The Process Church of the Final Judgment, according to Clarke, traces its origins back to London in 1957 with a group called Compagnia del Grane Morti, which believed in a millenarian apocalypse. By the late 1960s, influenced by nuclear fear and spiritual growth, the Process Church emphasized non-attachment to pride, sensuality, luxury, and wealth, promoting a gospel of peace. Unique aspects of the Process Church included its attempt to convert two different social classes, prolific literature production, controversial founder, and subsequent surge of conspiracy theories.

During the 1970s, the Church faced heightened controversy as high-profile celebrities declared affiliation, leading to sensationalist press and a United States Congressional investigation into its tax-exempt status. Rumors of Satanic involvement and international conspiracy further fueled the Church's notoriety. The Process Church serves as an intriguing case study for Religious Studies scholars, shedding light on millenarian groups, mainstream reactions to cults, and the intersection of religion and conspiracy theory.

The Process Church of the Final Judgment was founded by British ex-Scientologists Anne and Robert DeGrimston, who attracted followers from both those interested in Scientology and those opposed to it. They established a unique organization dedicated to exploring the duality of good and evil, attracting attention and speculation due to their charismatic leadership and ambiguous activities. While some former members described the leaders as not living up to their psychopathic image, others portrayed them as sociopathic murderers and gangsters. The Process Church defied easy categorization, drawing from various religious views and operating as a cult-like organization during the 1960s and 1970s.

In the 21st century, the Process Church's legacy fueled fascination and paranoia about potential criminal or conspiratorial elements within religious groups, leading to a proliferation of conspiracy theories. Its influence in popular culture, combined with its enigmatic presentation, captured the imagination of many, contributing to the belief in exaggerated conspiracy theories about the group's activities and supposed supernatural abilities. Despite these sensationalized narratives, the true extent of the Process Church's influence and activities remains elusive.

The Process Church of the Final Judgment was founded in the mid-1960s by three individuals who were former members of the Church of Scientology. They aimed to create a new religious movement that synthesized elements of Christianity and Satanism, viewing God and Satan as complementary forces within a unified cosmology. They sought to address the duality within the human soul and the conflicting portrayals of God and Satan. Their beliefs were outlined in their grand tome, "The Book of the Coming Forth by Light," which emphasized the integration of faith in God with self-understanding and insight into Satan.

The Process Church of the Final Judgment operated with a hierarchical structure, divided into four levels of teachings or stages, based on the individual's level of responsibility and awareness. Individuals typically began as readers before progressing to servants and then magistrates, with each stage requiring a significant time commitment for development. Weekly Sunday rituals served as a central event, fulfilling both religious and social functions, and fostering group cohesion. While not an organized religion with a dedicated building, the Process Church maintained formal meetings and an informal hierarchy to facilitate group therapy, socialization, and discussion of theological concepts. This structure allowed members to maintain contact, discuss publications, and explore the implications of their beliefs in the real world, as envisioned by the founders.

The Process Church of the Final Judgment maintained that individuals who became interested in their teachings did so through personal decision-making, contrary to allegations of aggressive recruitment tactics. While some authorities, like the Attorney General of Massachusetts, viewed the organization as cunning and successful in attracting members, the Church emphasized instilling a sense of purpose and mission in its followers. However, former members have reported experiences of aggressive recruitment efforts, including methods like canvassing, advertising, word of mouth, and transportation to meeting places. The perception of the Process Church as a "recruiting cult" with coercive tactics has contributed to its controversial image, despite claims that potential members approached the community voluntarily.

The Process Church of the Final Judgment experienced a significant increase in the dissemination of its teachings, leading to a surge in membership from 30,000 subscribers to at least 200,000 eager learners. However, as public perception shifted, the relevance of the Church's insights and implementations diminished, with increased questioning and resistance to its proposed life application, centered around concepts like the Ubermensch and animal identities. Despite attempts to focus on mundane details of the organization's hierarchy, rumors persisted of secretive super-authorities guiding the group from the top.

The legacy of the Process Church is complex, marked by intense scrutiny and speculation about its connections to other organizations. Although research has both validated and disapproved of these connections, the organization faced challenges, including infiltration by groups like The Fund for the Investigation of Cults, leading to negative stigma and altered materials. However, some genuine prophecies and experiences persisted, maintaining the intrigue surrounding the Process Church's enigmatic history.

Following the official dissolution of The Process Church in 1974, members of its four sects have continued to promote compassionate values and contribute positively to their communities. Some former members have established successful animal-assisted therapy groups, with one group even conducting sessions at a prestigious hospital. Reflective joy and fond memories of their time in the organization characterize recent meetings among former members, highlighting the positive experiences many had during their involvement. Spokespersons from various branches of The Process have shared stories of love and kindness with the media, emphasizing the enduring impact of the organization's teachings.

Despite the dissolution, members of all four sects have embraced their teachings to lead meaningful lives and contribute to society. They have pursued careers in counseling, art, activism for animal welfare, and advocacy for love and compassion. Through various mediums such as books, educational materials, and personal actions, former members continue to spread the message of love and empathy, inspiring others to join their cause.

The influence of the Process Church of the Final Judgment extends into contemporary esoteric religion, particularly under the concept of "forces" theology, which posits two equal but opposite deities merging into a unified god. This dualistic framework directly reflects Process dualism and has been embraced by theologians such as Starhawk, Zsuzsanna Budapest, Robert E. Svoboda, and Margot Adler. Additionally, Haitian Voodoo has incorporated forces theology into its syncretic cosmology, while even within the Catholic Church, theologians like Hans Küng have been influenced by Process ideas. Despite its marginal status and dissolution in the 1970s, the Process Church's impact on esoteric and theological thought persists, shaping contemporary understandings of spirituality and religious practice.

The Process Church of the Final Judgment, founded by Robert and Mary Baker in 1963, was a controversial new religious movement known for its teachings, practices, and enigmatic members. Despite being misunderstood and subject to moral panics, it attracted individuals from diverse backgrounds who were drawn to its message of surrendering the ego, promoting service, and wrestling with inner demons. The community provided holistic experiences and empowered fearful individuals through relationships and a temporary socio-economic structure. Despite the myths and legends surrounding the group's affiliation with the 'dark underbelly' of society, the reality was often different, with members contributing equally to the community and benefiting from its support and security. Even after almost 60 years, the Process Church remains a subject of intrigue and speculation, shaping society's collective consciousness.

The Finders Case and
Allegations of Child Abuse

The "Finders" case of the 1980s remains a haunting enigma in the realm of child abuse investigations, characterized by a web of allegations, speculations, and controversies. This paper delves into the intricate details of the case, shedding light on the origins of the Finders group, the allegations of child abuse, the ensuing investigations, and the enduring questions surrounding potential CIA involvement.

The Finders was a purported New Age group founded in the 1960s, known for its unconventional beliefs and lifestyle centered around communal living and alternative spirituality.

In 1987, the Tallahassee Police Department initiated an investigation into allegations of child abuse involving members of the Finders group. Disturbing reports emerged of children being subjected to neglect, physical abuse, and exploitation while under the care of the group.

Law enforcement agencies in Florida and Washington, D.C. conducted thorough investigations into the allegations of child abuse. The discovery of documents detailing child trafficking and exploitation heightened concerns about the group's activities.

Speculation emerged regarding potential ties between the Finders group and the Central Intelligence Agency (CIA). Allegations suggested that the CIA may have utilized the group for intelligence-gathering purposes, leading to suspicions of a cover-up of their illicit activities.

"The Finders," revelations about activities in Iran-Contra and similar illicit operations were made during the same time as the "Finders" Case. Psychologist Peter Brown reports information from an unknown man in 2004 who warned him about the intelligence and crime connections for the Waco, Texas Branch Davidian disaster where over 70 men, women, and children were killed in a fire. An officer was accused of inappropriate contact with relatives or members of Todashev. There was an unexpected death of the man who killed Todashev. Lobbying perpetrated by the Center and citizens started when Todashev was shot by one or more officers. The administrators of the world police surveillance state, who seek to deny citizens a strong lobby by orchestrating confusion and images of incompetence.

CIA Involvement - The "Finders" had gained influence due to their promised management of and technical expertise in the then early computer field with the most secret telecommunication affiliations with the U.S. CIA seeking to conceal their activities. These actions suggest that different U.S. intelligence agencies such as the FBI, pressured by witnesses of drug activity involving Todashev or Hall's offers of FBI protection for this same drug trafficking, may have already known of the true nature of "The Finders" and cooperated to conceal their activities independently. "The Finders" are suspected of offenses of human and child trafficking, murder, abuse, child pornography, and secret service roles in the U.S. Federal government.

The most considerable link between the "Finders" and the government is the CIA links. Multiple investigation documents by the Tallahassee and U.S. Customs Services division draw this same conclusion. Before any official response was made, the first search warrant was executed by the D.C. Police to investigate child abuse allegations. Keys to six rental property locations in Tallahassee, Florida, elsewhere in Florida and Alabama, and to the communes and warehouses in Washington were found. They also found verified cult leader Marion David Pettie (also known as "The Game Caller"). Pettie, his Vietnamese "wife," and four Finders had to be released when it was found that the Tallahassee police had improperly executed the search warrant. The Federal Bureau of Investigation, who was categorized as taking no action, requested copies of this search warrant return.

Clearly, much more is going on than just a simple case of some accused child molesters. The observation by several case observers that this could be a 'homestead family' utilizing an alternative lifestyle was a point of view expressed much earlier in the case and has little standing in light of what has since come to light. At the other extreme are those that hold that the techniques used are consistent with intelligence agency covens. There is just too little evidence to come to conclusions about these specific people. However, much about the process of setting up covers and the expected CIA response as not a crime, surveillance, are consistent with accusations of CIA employ. It cannot be allowed to be overlooked as this investigation proceeds that these were the tools of the CIA unless credible evidence is found to the contrary.

Unfortunately, as in Sections 3.1 and 3.3, it is still unclear how valuable secondary sources are and whether their authors have relied on the same primary material to an acceptable degree. It's also noteworthy that the author of an unrelated CCOSA report that is often cited to point to a CIA involvement in possible child abuse within certain circles based their speculation on another source document they've been able to review. That report also features a number of additional original observations and it offers secondary material in the form of outside sources; however, the indices of the primary material (the FOI documents) themselves, thus lending firmness to its conclusions, have not been released thus far. Ultimately, reliance on secondary material has to be especially cautionary given that the phenomenon in question, alleged child abuse within the Finders cult, on which the national press in the USA has reported out of sources which lie within direct distance from the case, has at times been dismissed as nonexistent while investigators have been accused of being part of a witch-hunt.

Although theories of a military and/or intelligence agency's involvement have been widespread and heavily emphasized by certain circles in the media and especially by conspiracy researchers since the beginning of the Finders investigation, the actual claims of CIA involvement in the case, maintained over the years in various secondary sources primarily by anecdotal evidence and some uncritically interpreted FOIA documents, have been very vague, never explicitly verifiable, and without specific individuals named, tested, or put to the thesis "ad portas". Now we have the opportunity to check them, using partly the same sources that are usually available in the Finders literature and partly newly released FOIA documents. The expectation should probably be that within our legal framework they'll produce the same vague and unverifiable results. Hence secondary information has to be of special significance in this case.

Keys to moving the investigation of the Finders ahead may lie in efforts to return the Finders' melody making, database assembling capacities to more proper goals. To resolve what was really going on with the Finders, we need to look at the bigger picture. People have been identified. The potential for a genuine and most timely remedy is a real possibility. Instead of accusing offenders through legal channels that have been obviously co-opted by their oversight, the executive, legislative, and judicial branches of government, through its Constitutional authority and obligation, can and must investigate and act directly. This is the purpose and guarantee of the rule of law - an obligation to seek truth and redress with fairness and in the best interests of all people. In the wake of many otherwise unfathomable crimes, this truth is rising. Those in authority should act to ensure that this truth means something more than just explaining why they have not allowed the authority they have to be implemented.

After the Justice Department concluded that the children's allegations about satanic ritual abuse were false, they were returned to their mothers and the evidentiary trial regarding the Finders ended. The investigation ceased abruptly. Why? What exactly did the U.S. Customs Service find? Was there sufficient evidence of illegal activity to go to trial? If the children were indeed well cared for, why were the men charged with child abuse in the first place? If there was no child abuse, why was the investigation ended rather than deepened? What or who was being protected? Many unanswered questions remain. It is hoped that this thoroughly researched article has provided enough information so that a credible investigation might be resumed. This time it should not involve any agency whose peripheral involvement in the case may prevent a clear view of the central one.

CIA and MP force involvement in the Finders investigation only inflated the size of the problem. Although there is no evidence to justify a CIA conspiracy, the image of the CIA as a secret and all-powerful entity that can stage manage or cover up an incident is certainly familiar within the public's generally cynical view of intelligence activities. It is unfortunate that otherwise reliable parties did not look closer before pronouncing conclusions on slim evidence or hearsay. It's time to dispel the fog from the Finders investigation. After numerous interviews and trips back and forth to Florida and Virginia, disturbing allegations and conspiracies have proved to be largely unfounded. Was a critic right when stating that "Conspiracy thinking, by offering a popular understanding of all the world's evils, effectively reassures us that there's no real connection between those evils"? In the Finders case, perhaps not. But those who consider conspiracies as scapegoats following the inability to comprehend fact should not believe that exposing and disbanding a few conspiracy theories will have an impact. The skeptical concept persists. The key requirement today is the public's continued support for excellent law enforcement organizations - and that will require continuous visibility and outreach for these organizations.

The investigation concluded there were erroneous early reports that the Finders were involved in a well-organized, large-scale child abuse operation - raising the specter that a cult ritual might be involved. Over time, authorities could identify only six children who were actual Finders, and these children seemed well cared for and properly educated - not physically or emotionally abused. The investigation concluded there was no evidence that the children involved in the Finders case had been sexually abused, had been used as child prostitutes, or had been subjected to Satanism. Nevertheless, first impressions can be like cement. They weigh heavily in the public's mind, and early reports keep resurfacing, regardless of how inaccurate they are.

The case garnered significant media attention, sparking public outrage and calls for accountability. However, the complexities of the case and the involvement of federal agencies fueled conspiracy theories and controversies.

Despite extensive investigations, no charges related to child abuse were ultimately filed against members of the Finders group. The lack of prosecutions left many unanswered questions and unresolved suspicions surrounding the case.

vulnerabilities of children to exploitation and the challenges of investigating complex cases of child abuse. It underscored the need for enhanced child protection measures and improved coordination among law enforcement agencies.

Decades later, the Finders case continues to fuel speculation and conspiracy theories, with unanswered questions about the group's activities and potential ties to intelligence agencies lingering in the public consciousness.

The Finders case remains a haunting reminder of the complexities and challenges inherent in investigating allegations of child abuse, particularly when intertwined with speculation about intelligence agency involvement. While the specifics of the case may remain shrouded in mystery, its legacy underscores the importance of vigilance in protecting vulnerable children and seeking accountability for those who exploit them.

The Rise and Fall of Jeffrey Epstein

If someone could design a perfect template to believe in conspiracy theories, they would be hard-pressed to do better than what happened in the Epstein case. The arrest and subsequent suicide of the 66-year-old financier and convicted sex offender still haunt the public. Jeffrey Epstein's alleged sexual proclivities dominated the U.S. news cycle in the summer of 2019 as the wealthy sex offender and industrious socialite had frequent and friendly contacts with a range of political figures, establishment personalities, and celebrities. Before his 2019 arrest, Epstein was already a controversial figure due to various allegations of sexual misconduct. He maintained—and often cultivated—serviceable relations with different political figures, even though his 2008 criminal record for soliciting prostitution of a minor had resulted in a controversial plea deal. After serving only 13 months out of an 18-month sentence in the private wing of the Palm Beach County Jail, Epstein underwent a rehabilitation process, and he reemerged as a much-sought fundraising figure before he was remanded into federal custody.

Since his 2019 indictment by federal authorities and the alleged suicide of former financier and convicted sex offender Jeffrey Epstein, Epstein has been at the center of a web of conspiracy and cover-up. This conspiracy is baroque and straddles political, financial, and academic boundaries. Conspiracy theories flourish in any population bereft of information. The public's ignorance or skepticism about the facts fosters the creation of myths by powerful entities interested in obfuscating the truth. Various events or narrative discrepancies may undermine these theories, or they may be further bolstered by the perception by multiple people that actual events could support the existence of a conspiracy. Often, conspiracy can have a remarkable appeal to individuals who have been socially marginalized and consequently are reluctant to accept the explanations offered by the establishment for mainstream events. Moreover, the rapid dissemination of conspiracy theories has been enabled by the development of social media technologies that connect and amplify fringe voices who believe in unsupported ideas.

Meanwhile, following Epstein's death, U.S. Attorney General William Barr declared to Congress that Epstein's death resulted from a combination of thwacks. Later, Dr. Michael Baden (a New York City Chief Medical Examiner) pronounced that Epstein died from homicidal violence against his person. Less than a week after Epstein's death, the United States opted to arrest the two postal guards on duty the night the inmate died.

The Metropolitan Correctional Centre in New York City is considered one of the best correctional facilities in the United States. Nonetheless, somehow, while he was there, Epstein experienced an untimely suicide on August 10, 2019. His jailers, it seemed, were deeply neglectful at best and violating both standards and their systemic aims at worst. For the next few months, the mainstream narratives surrounding Epstein and his affairs included conversations about jailers failing to monitor him, videotape data that were accidentally deleted (or another excuse, for which there were at least three or four), and phone-operated security cameras that malfunctioned, while the server housing the footage was in a disreputable state of being.

In 2019, law enforcement seemed to reverse history when they claimed newly charged crimes by Epstein justified his denial of bail. It was a brief incarceration. Epstein died in his prison cell, awaiting trial for sex trafficking for voluntary purposes. His death metamorphosed into din as the public consumed the happenstance surrounding it.

In 2005, Palm Beach law enforcement began investigating claims that Jeffrey Epstein and British socialite Ghislaine Maxwell were sexually abusing minor females. Soon, over 40 women came forward with complaints against Epstein. An 11-month investigation by the Palm Beach Police Department concluded that Epstein should be charged with one count of sexual activity with a minor, four counts of lewd and lascivious molestation, and one count of solicitation of prostitution. These allegations resulted in two solicitations of minor charges and one felony count of solicitation of prostitution against Epstein. He ended up in prison, serving only 13 months of an 18-month sentence. This series of events would become a source of scandal and controversy in American law and the American public conversation during the years to come.

The school of philosophy believes that a political conspiracy makes sense only if it contains a sexual one, namely tantric sex, at its core. We argue that tensions in tantra and unfulfilled commitments would serve as maintainers of secrecy. In Eastern spirituality, tantra means "Transcendental Network". In the prince's generation, an aristocrat had emergency access to the king only to take part in a tantric sexual rite. Osho Rajneesh even ties tantra to a story of the main Harlot of Babylon. In politics, tantra may have signified the maintenance of the sacred bond between the god and the devotees, which serves to avoid political breakdown. According to Vedas, Tantra rules that under the conditions of modernity (Kali Yuga), one must enter into a sexual bond to achieve any results. The concept of lewd, promiscuous sex is foreign to many. It is mainly manifested by a sadist who exploits his rank or any other sacred duty to manipulate and inflict suffering at will to prove his absolute power.

The purpose of this article is to provide insight into and model an intricate elite sex cult that is believed to be operating as an additional layer of power in a conspiracy with global reach. The secondary purpose of this article is to achieve academic expert evaluation and recognize the importance of the reported phenomenon. The indicated secondary problem is also the primary method of investigation. We believe our model of the operating elite sex cult provides a new angle of insight into the recent Jeffrey Epstein scandal and a general segment of conspiracy research potentiality.

The preparations made and steps that are anticipated to be taken about the recent arrest of Jeffrey Epstein were allegedly likely to have been found in court. Earlier this year, authorities executed a search warrant and took flash drives with them. Epstein did not yet know that he would be indicted for federal crimes. Numerous items of fascination were aboard the drives taken in the search. Despite being equipped with spy or hidden recording devices and equipment designed to track and record cloud-stored communications, there was not enough satisfaction in that data alone. There is not enough evidence to confirm that the allegations here are accurate. Neither is there reason to think they are untrue. How could the general thrust of the allegations be so if something relevant to conspirators being investigated was found earlier this year? Authorities did not even know the elements of the indictment they were to file, to say nothing of having to initiate a tactic to gather embarrassing pictures and information on a Federal judge.

The scope of criminal conduct alleged in the Epstein indictment is more than ample. Epstein is said to have been employing young girls to engage in commercial sex acts. Some of these were sexually exploited on his properties. Some were also sexually exploited by his clients - adult men with wealth and power who knew that the females involved were children. This case will be of high profile due to the fame and wealth of the alleged enterprise's associated clientele. Suppose journalists, online commentators, and court spectators correctly say behind-the-scenes widespread conspiracy would not constitute a crime against the public. In that case, those serving the public will not likely be apt to care what documents were to be found lying around in the hands of a freedom of information request. Thank the public and student body for being alert to the story and expressing when there is a need for a court that is serious about paying attention to the complaint. If it takes the public to publicize the substantial allegations here successfully, then the public will have stood for their rights.

There are also many other supporters of the accused. Sandy and Sophie Baños, Chantal Biancato, Lisa Cohen, Ricky Cohen, Laura Goldman, Nancy K. Larkins, Shannon McCullough, David Rodgers, Jorge Scientific Corp., Pop & Partners, Arrow, SSCVC Corporation, and Northwest Hemispheric LLC have all been mentioned as involved on the side of the accused. Two of Fallon's and Connolly's close associates, Fred Fielding, who was President Nixon's lawyer (the person responsible for convincing him to retain the evidence contained on the tapes of the president's phone calls), and a former Secretary of The Treasury, Lawrence Summers (former chief economist of The World Bank and Secretary of The Treasury under President Clinton), are also implicated. Former Harvard president Larry Summers was accused at the time by then-Harvard student Andrew Crespo of failing to address allegations of sexual assault against a professor during an internal investigation as an attempt to obstruct a related legal case. Both Brown and Barney Frank criticized Harvard for its failure to address sexual misconduct allegations while accusing Summers of misleading them about his actions in cases of sexual assault at Harvard.

In the cases of Jeffrey Epstein and Ghislaine Maxwell, numerous key players are working with Epstein and his co-conspirators or other relevant parties. Epstein's close associates, Isabel Maxwell, Jean-Luc Brunel, and Les Wexner, have been mentioned in numerous accounts of the criminal activities in Epstein's orbit. Key figures involved directly in attempts to obstruct justice, intimidate victims, cover up the extent of the crimes, and secure Epstein's release from jail (before his death) include Epstein's lawyers: Alan Dershowitz, Darren K. Indyke, Richard D. Kahn, Martin Weinberg, and Maria Farmer (among others). Supporters like Spencer Kuvin and Bradley Edwards (co-counsel in the Florida case) act as counter-agents assisting on behalf of the victims.

The objective was to avoid making direct payments from Epstein's accounts. During the period of the conspiracy, the defendants sent more than $35,000,000 in 1,150 wires and 1,100 checks to men and women who were allegedly trafficking conspiracy. The defendants' messengers frequently used correspondent bank accounts of correspondent banks located there to avoid direct connections between Epstein and the expenditures. To further insulate Epstein, his employees, and his agents who participated in the transfer of payments, the defendants sought to oversee the use of WhatsApp and encrypted conducted business email addresses, providing instructions on how to pay money and the fake titles used. To further send money to victims, conspirators encouraged them to seek additional Davalos advantage from Epstein's legal advisors and payment recipients.

The hidden offshore financial vehicles, secret relationships, and nefarious activities stoked conspiracy theories of all kinds. According to the indictment by the Southern District of New York office of Bali Cables Limited, between February 1, 2000, and the present, numerous individuals conspired to operate a massive multi-million-dollar scheme: setting up direct payments to conceal not only the source but also the nature of the payments by Epstein. One method to hide and disguise the payments was to label them as administrative or consulting fees, among other legitimate-sounding services or expenses. False and fraudulent entries and acronyms were used on financial case reports to mislead the persons or companies to which they were directed regarding the true purpose of the conventional transfers. The conspiracy members also sent the money through deadly or shell companies with no legitimate business operations or minimal or purely token business operations.

To fully crystallize the different strands of a conspiracy, we need convincing evidence that Jeffrey Epstein and other individuals involved in the same criminal conspiracy acted with a common purpose or strong implication among its different parts and that this remained so throughout the conspiracy. The material already on file concerns deeds that would have occurred since early 2002 but might go back further into the past. Statements, including exculpatory statements by third parties with or without reason before that time and pertaining even remotely to the deeds, could provide additional such evidence. Statements might also indicate that the "fertilization" of the criminal construct through real estate and other public and private transactions and the re-routing of proceeds following the international real estate downturn would have been apparent or was again present. With more proof, a broader or different mix of criminal hypocrisy could surface, possibly negative proof. Ongoing credibility concerns vis-à-vis important NGOs may or may not be allayed if French authorities arrest or refuse to cooperate in furthering the proceedings against a person or persons present at the birth of the criminal project.

Before or by the time justice authorities became aware of Jeffrey

Epstein's many organized criminal activities, they had long become accustomed to making cover-up decisions concerning powerful sex abusers, especially in the U.S. It also appears that significant events, e.g., a new criminal case, hearing, or trial, seemed to dovetail with critics' concentrated efforts to highlight specific issues, thus temporarily sidelining these. Epstein himself was not the only one to die under suspicious circumstances in that case. His private money launderer was involved in the vehicle in the alleged trafficking of many prominent and influential persons. Not everyone would have appreciated being put in a position similar to that of the Queen, according to Epstein.

Epstein and the claimants have never questioned the reliability of Cooley's quote. To the contrary, the $1.4 million settlements with Cooley and Dentons' involvement with other claimants prevented the conspiracy from being submerged. OIG then collaborated with the Washington Legal Foundation in creating an association of class action law firms that participated in approximately the same non-Kissell as the third-party defendants. Pomeranz's email started. The third-party defendant Fredericks moved to take discovery on their Hindering Claims. In their Opposition, claimants argued that the allegations of the Third-Party Complaint did not state a claim for conspiracy with NCE. In discovery, Cooley produced emails and documents related to the legality of NCE transactions, where Cooley requested permission from the third-party defendants to respond to discovery requests with a protective order, and third-party defendants did not cooperate.

In their reply brief in Epstein, aggrieved investors opposed Epstein's arguments by stressing that his concession several months before in the Fraud Façade claim, that Bartko failed to plead the material misrepresentations in the Offerings affirmatively, hindered dismissal with leave to amend and saving grace by which his complaint could not be amended to allege the material misrepresentations and omissions in the Offerings. Again, the Epstein and Headwaters district court opinions are inconsistent with their conflicting reasoning of how a complaint should be amended to state a conspiracy claim.

Epstein's counterarguments to dismissing the case involve refuting nine of the reasons supplied by the court to justify ignoring the claim.

The argument is that the dismissal of the claim was plain error, as it used the wrong standard of review, and that, at worst, the complaint should be dismissed with leave to amend and limited to the non-Kissell class allegations. In exploring Epstein's counterarguments, some additional implications are raised, some of which I will now address.

Victims also suffer interpersonally. Agents of the system that downplay, ignore, or discourage them send not only a clear message to the survivors themselves but to loved ones as well: their pain does not matter. Such a message can result in feelings of betrayal, anger, and disconnection from the junction points that should function as protective buffers. If one listens to the survivors' needs and the loved ones' wishes, any justice process should be imbued with therapeutic qualities. Lastly, the institutional response to calls of conspiracy and cover-up forms some of the most problematic implications. Given how allegations of conspiracy can be damaging, it is essential to remember that the proliferation of such claims are facts of extrinsic origin, behaviors typically becoming apparent when the actions of wrongdoers do not make sense.

The adverse effects on victims and survivors whenever information is altered, deleted, or hidden are related to such actions' meanings. In other words, obstruction of justice sends the message that survivors' voices are meaningless, making it likely that they become disillusioned and discouraged. Also, doubt that arises can compound survivors' self-doubt and feelings of guilt. Furthermore, from their view, the broader community does not value justice since, if it did, they would not have had their experiences taken away. Yet their feelings and reactions about attempts to conceal information are also important because a good level of mental health is linked to an individual's ability to assert oneself and to have enough agency to make a difference. Thus, downplaying, ignoring, and discouraging advocacy efforts can serve to limit opportunities for healing and growth. Finally, a lack of trust in institutions prevents or stalls cooperation and increases the likelihood of pushing survivors away, thereby reinforcing isolation.

Epstein's death increased those feelings of distrust and anger. Over the past few decades, conspiracy theories have been on the uptick for a variety of reasons. One important justification is the decline in the prestige of experts and public institutions as authoritative mediators of knowledge and truth. When the public stops trusting what official accounts and narratives tell, it is more difficult to challenge those who use the narrative to articulate their opinions or documents like public policies. Suspicion of the official account can give rise to narratives that, sometimes, go even deeper in the distrust of the institutional narrative by calling for the complicity of external actors. These are conspiracy narratives. It is in this framework that conspiracy theories become vehicles to legitimize alternative explanations if official narratives are no longer constrained to be respected, thanks to their acknowledged credibility. Three arguments contribute to increasing the allure of conspiracy theories for explaining official events: epistemic and psychological.

To compound these problems, the Jeffrey Epstein suicide immediately gave rise to an even more severe crisis of public trust and confidence in the United States and elsewhere, not unwarrantedly due to doubts on issues like those mentioned before. Since credibility and public trust are scarce commodities in democratic societies, their debasement turned a bad situation into an even worse predicament. Society is already suffering from a crisis of public trust and confidence in many areas of scientific knowledge, including medicine, climate change, and public health programs. In fact, these are just different facets of a generalized societal loss of authority and respect for institutions and organizations that usually wield the power to delineate what we know as "truth." Authorities can no longer say "trust us" and expect the members of society to accept and comply with their interpretations and recommendations. Authorities must be able to listen and respond to the needs, aspirations, and concerns of the members of society and incorporate them into their designs, thus earning and maintaining the public's trust.

Researchers and organizations committed to research ethics point out that child sexual abuse is basically a crime that occurs under the cover of darkness. According to estimates, less than 20% of criminal acts are reported to law enforcement, and only a small proportion of these reports lead to even an investigation and much less a satisfactory criminal penalty. In the large part of the iceberg below the surface, the maltreatment goes on, often causing more apparent damage and for a longer period than the criminal procedures' negative side effects. Retraction, even those motivated by genuine mistakes in the courtroom, usually bans the media from informing the public about what the allegations in the indictment initially were and, therefore, about what the journalists had been reporting or not been reporting. Statements like "the yellow press whipped up a scandal" violate the reporting ban and the courts' image-build intentions, triggering strict measures.

Public figures' reactions during the Epstein affair, such as their befriending or defense of Epstein, as well as alleged or proven involvement, were damaging not only for them but also for the important figures and works they represent. Viewers started to see the institution as a whole as a supporter or perpetrator of these deeds. Indeed, two members of the British Royal Family distanced themselves from the public eye after the scandal; one of them did at least temporarily withdraw as a foreign trade envoy shortly after Epstein's then-most recent child-prostitution-related conviction, and the other member declined to follow another normal activity after the scandal, not even to attend his close relative's funeral. In a written response to a journalist's question, the late Otto von Habsburg, formerly an MEP and head of a dynasty formerly ruling in Hungary, said that this image-generating effect of cover-up attempts applies not only to them but also to "all general and alumni relations with money," and that would explain his unwillingness to get involved in any charity activity.

Also, in response to an order made by the district court, the attorney filed an addendum detailing Epstein-related investigations and further potential victims. The estate has also filed an application with the district court seeking permission to engage in alternative dispute resolution with the Epstein victims, all represented through various law firms. According to the district attorney, there are ongoing investigations into the crimes of the defendants. Following several orders, the DOJ released an Epstein-related inner-law enforcement investigatory document on August 19, 2020. The district attorney for Palm Beach County, Florida, issued an April 2011 Report of Investigation to Consolidate Interviews, but the U.S. DOJ and the U.S. attorney determined that the transparency interest does not outweigh the need for secrecy.

Various lawsuits have been filed, including against Epstein's estate and its beneficiaries, seeking compensatory and punitive damages, reimbursement of costs and attorney's fees, injunctions, and declaratory relief. Individual lawsuits, at least in the beginning, were consolidated by the Judicial Panel on Multidistrict Litigation with the United States District Court for the Southern District of New York under MDL No. 2923. The prosecution has taken several steps to investigate and prosecute Jeffrey Epstein and his co-conspirators. Several federal judges have also conducted fact-findings. There is an ongoing DOJ investigation into Epstein's plea agreement, focusing on the role of Alex Acosta.

In line with the #MeToo moment, using Epstein as a platform to encourage victims against powerful men may drive societal shifts. Permitting court-ordered immunity breached crime victims' rights. Moreover, the silence was defeated as girlfriends, protection laws, the House of Representatives, and attention-seeking victims united parties, territories, and social movements. In sum, public outrage may induce state and federal criminal charges and civil actions against enablers. Furthermore, public opinion and outrage may well shape fashion, homelessness, depression, and the legislative histories of collaborative agreements. Legal history and case law underscore this research's timeliness, relevance, and continuing importance.

Support for conspiracy allegations may induce public outrage and demand for justice. The Jeffrey Epstein case illustrates negative public reactions to conspiracy allegations. His 2019 arrest sparked headlines and public anger against a powerful abuser who received a slap on the wrist in Florida despite evidence of child sex trafficking. Conspiracy allegations further fueled anger at prosecutors and demands for justice. Indeed, conspiracy may illustrate proof of public opinion's disapproval and societal changes. Public outrage may drive legal reviews. Public calls for disqualification may occur to disbarred lawyers. Sweeping appellate and Supreme Court decisions may result in limited actions and agreements. Publicizing the evidence against child molesters and abusers may aid victims and pre-victims.

The Jeffrey Epstein scandal has left an indelible mark on society, serving as a stark reminder of the corruption and abuse of power that can thrive among the elite. This paper delves into the intricate details of the Epstein case, examining the allegations of conspiracy and cover-up surrounding his demise. Furthermore, it underscores the imperative need for transparency, accountability, and justice in addressing crimes of exploitation and abuse.

Ghislaine Maxwell's Sex Trafficking Victims' Justice and Accountability

As Ghislaine Maxwell faces trial for her alleged involvement in Jeffrey Epstein's sex trafficking ring, the world watches closely, recognizing the significance of this moment in the pursuit of justice. This paper delves into the pivotal nature of Maxwell's trial, emphasizing the importance of holding perpetrators accountable, the role of evidence and public demand, and the implications for victims of sex trafficking.

Maxwell is accused of aiding and abetting Epstein's sex trafficking operation, which includes the recruitment and exploitation of underage girls. These allegations underscore the severity of her alleged crimes and the need for accountability.

Maxwell's trial represents a crucial moment in the quest for justice for Epstein's victims and sheds light on the systemic abuse perpetrated within elite circles. The outcome of this trial will reverberate far beyond the courtroom, shaping perceptions of accountability and the protection of vulnerable individuals.

The outcome of Maxwell's trial hinges significantly on the evidence she possesses, including any documentation or testimony that may implicate other individuals involved in the trafficking ring. The credibility and thoroughness of the evidence presented will be instrumental in determining the trial's outcome.

In the aftermath of Epstein's scandal, there has been a surge in public demand for accountability. The scrutiny surrounding Maxwell's trial reflects a broader societal expectation for transparency and justice, compelling authorities to conduct a comprehensive investigation and ensure that all responsible parties are accountable.

Accountability is paramount for upholding the rule of law and demonstrating that no one is above it, regardless of their status or influence. Holding Maxwell accountable sends a clear message that those who engage in exploitation and abuse will face consequences for their actions.

For survivors of sex trafficking, the trial represents an opportunity for validation, closure, and healing. Seeing perpetrators held accountable validates survivors' experiences and affirms their right to justice, providing a sense of empowerment and validation.

By holding Maxwell accountable, society sends a strong message that exploitation and abuse will not be tolerated. This serves as a deterrent to potential perpetrators, signaling that there will be severe consequences for those who engage in such heinous crimes.

Maxwell's trial offers victims of Epstein's sex trafficking ring a chance to seek closure and healing from the trauma they endured. The legal proceedings provide an opportunity for survivors to confront their abuser and reclaim their sense of agency.

The trial has the potential to shift power dynamics, allowing survivors to reclaim control over their narratives and hold perpetrators accountable. This represents a significant step towards dismantling systems of exploitation and empowering survivors to assert their rights.

Maxwell was taken into custody by the Federal Bureau of Investigation (FBI), which had been tracking her through New Hampshire, where she had retreated during the COVID-19 outbreak. A New York grand jury indicted her on July 2, 2020, following a months-long investigation into allegations of abuse involving Jeffrey Epstein. The indictment charged her with six federal crimes, four of which are related to facilitating Epstein's sexual abuse of minor girls between 1994 and 1997. They occurred at Epstein's homes in New York City, Palm Beach, Florida, Santa Fe, New Mexico, and Maxwell's residence in London. The two others, charges of perjury, are the result of statements she made under oath, specifically that she did not know about Epstein's criminal behavior. If convicted, Ghislaine Maxwell faces up to 35 years in prison.

In the United States v. Maxwell, an indictment charged Ghislaine Maxwell with conspiracy to entice a minor to travel to engage in illegal sex acts; three substantive counts of enticing a minor to travel to engage in unlawful sex acts; conspiracy to transport a minor with the intent to engage in criminal sexual activity; and two substantive counts of transporting a minor with the intent to engage in criminal sexual activity. For her alleged involvement in Jeffrey Epstein's ongoing sex-trafficking operation, she committed perjury, lying in depositions taken in connection with the Epstein case. This article outlines the evidence prosecutors have amassed in their case against Maxwell and the defenses she is expected to raise.

On July 2, 2020, Ghislaine Maxwell was arrested by the United States (U.S.) Federal Bureau of Investigation (FBI) agents at a 156-acre estate without incident in Bradford, New Hampshire. The New York City jail guards classified Maxwell as an extreme public danger or at risk of escaping due to Maxwell's enormous amount of foreign financial resources. Maxwell denied any involvement and has never admitted to any crimes, but the victims reported that she aided Epstein in grooming and abusing underage girls between 1994 and 1997. Consequently, the prosecution charged her with trafficking minors, and she was facing up to 45 years in prison. After her arrest, multiple sources reported that her arrest would also have severe implications for other high-profile figures such as Prince Andrew. Finally, in early July 2020, the U.K. government could not guarantee Maxwell's safety from the novel coronavirus at the Metropolitan Detention Centre in Brooklyn, but the request was denied. Less than a year later, on December 20, 2021, Maxwell was found guilty and was remanded for a court hearing scheduled for June 28, 2022.

Ghislaine Maxwell is a British socialite born on December 25, 1961. Maxwell is the youngest child of Betty and Sir Robert Maxwell, a Czechoslovakian-born British media and newspaper proprietor. Given her father's reputation as an unscrupulous businessman, Ghislaine Maxwell has been frequently referred to as the favorite child of the notorious press baron by the media and the public. Her father lost his life falling from his yacht, named Lady Ghislaine, and despite his net worth being estimated at around £400 million, Robert Maxwell's death was surrounded by controversy. Robert Maxwell had stolen hundreds of millions of pounds of his employees' pensions and suffered severe financial difficulties. Recent reports by her family members and Maxwell herself have suggested that her former friendship with the disgraced financier and convicted sexual offender, Jeffrey Epstein, has forever connected Maxwell with the impression of her father as an individual with a dark side.

From Neil Lewis's interviews with Epstein and Maxwell over a decade, information about them can be pieced together over time. The idea of repeated interviews over time is quite different from the standard practice of investigative reporting, which revolves around interviews done in person and on specific topics. With the Epstein - Maxwell - Ghislaine Maxwell story, multiple interviews produced clues that helped explain what was happening. Instead of interviewing victims about the mid-1990s, 2000s, or even the 2010s, the time meant for simple to compound stories to develop as new facts were uncovered, interviews with people familiar with victims and suspects, including friends, family, household staff, financial advisers, the police who looked for evidence of crime, and the staff at law enforcement offices around the country who either pursued criminal investigations or stopped cases down may be of the most interest.

The events that led to the July 2, 2020, arrest of Ghislaine Maxwell on charges related to the sex trafficking of minors. The first half of the paper provides an overview of the allegations and people and places associated with Maxwell's trajectory from a British heiress to an alleged criminal co conspirator. The paper sets out the known facts based on what was filed in Maxwell's case by the beginning of August 2020. This information relates to Maria Farmer, the first person to state that Maxwell trafficked her publicly; Leslie Groff, who was Epstein's second-in-command; Courtney Wild and Virginia Guiffre, the first woman to sue Maxwell for participating in sex trafficking for Jeffrey Epstein, former Palm Beach police chief Michael Reiter who tried to bring Epstein to justice, a man posing as Reiter's colleague who approached the mother of an Epstein victim and Citizen Kane, John K. Douglas of Investigative Research Group, who pretended to be a journalist so that he could threaten an attorney suing Epstein, Guiffre, and Maxwell.

The proposition suggests that the ability of the victims to be able to relocate witnesses involved in the alleged abuse of Epstein's properties could become more difficult due to Ghislaine Maxwell's release on bail. The difficulty for the victims is outlined, as Maxwell's witnesses are significantly more available and less impacted by the potential impact of their evidence. The impact that these circumstances have on whether or not these victims of Epstein's sex trafficking ring would be motivated to serve a comparable notice of claim to Epstein does not need any of Maxwell's potential guilty abuse. The impact of the sources suggests that it is very likely that many victims coming forward with claims of Epstein-related sexual abuse have weakened since Ghislaine Maxwell's bail release.

Ghislaine Maxwell played a big part in Jeffrey Epstein's scheme to provide for girls of various ages by enticing them over to Epstein's properties. Epstein had sexual abuse involved in an array of circumstances where they were paid significant amounts of money by Epstein, who often handed over the money himself. Cameras have been installed in various locations of Epstein's properties, including the massage rooms. Locating important witnesses involved in the abuse of Epstein's properties can be extremely hard for multiple reasons. Many of Epstein's victims are fearful of formally coming forward and accusing Epstein due to his power, influence, and close relationships with numerous prominent individuals.

Maybe Maxwell was providing girls for herself. Following the wisdom that we should not attribute to malice what could have been proposed by stupidity, or maybe for lack of alternative reasons, or being aware of her reputation, known affiliations, lifestyle, activities (running a charity related to ocean preservation) or villa on a 10,000-acre ranch, and even her work resume, the media seems to help in contributing to the conspiracy and aversive perception regardless of additional circumstantial evidence that suggests she might not have composed a sex cartel. Some parallels I will draw to the Faurisson Affair are fictional and satirical; other unfortunate ones point toward historical events. It is important to note that many of these are purely speculative and are written only to entertain a hypothetical thought experiment that seeks to bring more subtle issues concerning Ms. Maxwell's legal treatment in current court proceedings.

The heavy media coverage and exposure of all details of proceedings play an essential role in shaping the perception and opinion of the public. Many media articles about Ghislaine Maxwell and the Epstein scandal are available, all of which frame and present her in ways that control and shape the discourse and narrative. From all the readings that I have done on this case, it seems that most have already judged her. In this media coverage, she is framed in various ways as Ms. Ghislaine Maxwell, the conspirator, involved in as many cases of sexual abuse as the criminal Epstein. Yet, it is naive to assume that she must be as guilty as he was because she was involved. Let's consider some alternative scenarios: involvement of unequally culpable parties. Maxwell might have been heavily engaged on the procurement and grooming side but perhaps not on the actual abuse and sexual trafficking. This has already been stressed by her lawyer, who wants to emphasize that Epstein is to blame, not the parents or women who provided the girls to Epstein.

Full decriminalization supports wealthy buyers at the expense of vulnerable individuals. Refocusing financial resources toward the development of individuals and the dissolution of generational, socioeconomic oppression weakens the sex industry infrastructure. Additionally, leveraging systemic resources for holistic enforcement may help address the issue.

Meanwhile, those with resources, as demonstrated in the Maxwell allegations, not only engage, promote, and protect the behavior of wealthy and powerful individuals who purchase sex, but they also seem to use younger women of more modest means to lure other women engaged in the sex trade to provide services in exchange for money. In both instances, leveraging systemic inequalities for financial gain is exemplified. Arguably, many individuals purchase sex from minors due to an overwhelming patriarchal and hoarding culture, where wealth enables the subjugation of individuals with insecure income. Wealth is leveraged for sexual gain, and the resulting oppression is perpetuated across generations through the solicitation of youth and financially secure placements.

In this paper, we focus on those forced into sex trafficking as compelled participants who exchange sexual favors for money for a variety of reasons while also acknowledging those who tangentially participate. It is essential to seek systemic solutions that address the marginalization of vulnerable individuals and eliminate the need or desire to engage in commercial sex work. Overturning patriarchal and hoarding culture is a distinct task from ending commercial sex work.

Addressing wealth-based gender and class oppression is a complex matter that requires systemic-level change. Many advocate for the decriminalization of sex work and the removal of financial barriers towards the development of a sexually deprived, subjugated, and often financially dependent class of workers. Essentially, the exchange of sexual favors for money is typical and, for many, the only feasible solution due to systemic inequality.

This case is unique because it is the first time that women who said they were sexually abused and trafficked will be asked to testify at all stages of a criminal case related to their abuse. Courts must ensure that these victims, with their genuine concerns about their safety, trauma, and the harmful impact of their trials' outcomes, are subject to a fair criminal trial. The ruling also adds another layer of complexity and balancing considerations to the broader questions. Others are more ready for the alleged acts for compensatory purposes, and the necessary legal processes to allow those claims to proceed have been stalled because they are not considered genuine claimants due to their criminal records and the origins of their legal claims. Any settlement must consider the views and needs of the victims. It is also essential for the legal courts to be mindful of the victim's privacy and dignity. They and the district attorneys are given nearly all the strategies. This is a critical case where the stakes are so high for women and survivors of human trafficking. It's not just the suspects' behavior that is under the microscope. The general public also watches how the criminal justice system treats impacted women.

The arrest of Ghislaine Maxwell promises an opportunity for justice for Epstein's victims. We urge the department to take their investigations into the alleged criminal acts of Ghislaine Maxwell and others to their logical conclusion rather than pushing for a tepid deal that would lock in Maxwell's previous non-prosecution agreement and unlawfully silence victims. Any trial should closely follow the evidence, listen to victims, and result in a just outcome. It is essential to allow a criminal trial to go forward and for there to be an opportunity for the appropriate consequences for any criminal conduct. In addition, it is equally important to spell out the roles of other people who may have participated in or enabled Maxwell's alleged conduct. As attention turns to other potential defendants like Maxwell's friends, we urge federal pretrial and trial courts to follow the provisions of Adriana Santos and Zorro Construction. They should not obey laws that are not rooted in the law and must not undermine the many victims' credible statements.

Charged with multiple counts of conspiracy with and aiding and abetting the sex trafficking of a minor alongside her involvement in inappropriate sexual activities with three young girls, the trial is of a high-profile nature that has generated a significant amount of public interest that will ultimately remain her biggest challenge. The age of the allegations and the notoriety of her involvement in Epstein's offenses will be closely scrutinized by the public and the media. This amplification of the trial could impact the defendant's rights in the courtroom. For the defense, research has shown that pretrial publicity affects several aspects of criminal proceedings. In conjunction with other media stories surrounding the Epstein investigation and Maxwell's resulting trial, many articles have also discussed the dubious ways the two figures were either involved or enabled such horrific acts over such a long period.

After four years of fighting in court, two different prison sentences, and various bail reviews, in April, Ghislaine Maxwell was finally given a trial date of July 12, 2021. The multiple delays in scheduling the trial were mainly due to difficulties arranging six months of depositions and transcripts in conditions affected by the COVID-19 pandemic, which impacted all other scheduling timetables. Amid pandemic restrictions and associated travel challenges, Maxwell's lawyer raised issues on selecting an impartial jury, expressing that public opinion against Maxwell could also affect them. It was clear that it would not be easy to find people who were not in some way influenced by the press coverage. Major UK and U.S. news outlets have notably covered Maxwell's case since her arrest in July 2020 due to her connection to Jeffrey Epstein.

Ghislaine Maxwell pays a hefty sum for release on bail.

As Ms. Chestman makes clear, messages about the critical and uncomfortable ideological issues this trial is likely to raise should be seen through the criminal rather than the criminal justice process. Namely, "The trial represents an opportunity for the public to see and hear those who were victimized by Epstein and Maxwell—an education that can be used to advance public discourse about the dangers young people, particularly vulnerable young people, face from predators who can offer them something the young otherwise can't secure on their own." Another aspect of this educational process is "the fact that young girls and women were prostituted, and paid by older men for what amounts to abuse under the guise of being a 'relationship.'"

The pursuit of justice for Ms. Maxwell by prosecutors and her trial will have significant implications more generally for our fight to end child sex trafficking, especially because both are so rare. A murky cloud of privilege historically protects sexual predators, particularly the rich and powerful. Rarely mentioned is the significant threat that victims will be retaliated against by the trafficker. Yet, the Newark Star-Ledger Editorial got it right ("For those who don't know, the facts ..."): "There are about 25 million victims of human trafficking around the world, 70% of whom are women and girls, according to the International Labour Organization. Closer to home, a 2020 U.S. State Department report found that in 2019, about 11,000 victims were identified in the U.S. alone."

Ghislaine Maxwell's trial is not just a legal proceeding but a symbolic moment in the fight against sex trafficking and the pursuit of justice for survivors. By prioritizing evidence-based proceedings and responding to public demand for accountability, the trial has the potential to deliver a resounding message of solidarity, empowerment, and justice for victims of exploitation and abuse. It is imperative that society stands united in support of survivors and remains steadfast in its commitment to eradicating sex trafficking and holding perpetrators accountable.

Examining P. Diddy's Involvement in Trafficking

Controversies and scandals have long marred the music industry, and allegations of trafficking involving prominent figures like P. Diddy have further tarnished its reputation. This paper delves into the accusations against P. Diddy, examining the evidence, the context surrounding the allegations, and the implications for the entertainment industry. By critically analyzing the claims, we aim to illuminate the complexities of addressing trafficking in the music world and the importance of accountability and justice.

P. Diddy, also known as Sean Combs, is a renowned figure in the music industry, celebrated for his contributions as a rapper, producer, and entrepreneur. However, his career has been shadowed by allegations of trafficking, raising questions about his involvement in illicit activities. This paper explores the allegations against P. Diddy, unraveling the truth behind the accusations and their impact on the entertainment landscape.

One of the keys to watching, guiding, shading the "dark" entertainment masses, and monitoring a new breed of "nihilistic, anarchist Black people was the monitoring and turning of drugs imported from South East Asia into Europe. They "sweat" captagon on some of the everything pushes, including its sales and celebrity users, an investigation that might yield fat profits for some drugs, per the F.B.I.'s reasoning. Puffy Combs was the person who offered this kind of help. Of Ivorian and Indo-Portuguese descent, his father had been a street warrior during the pre-Biafran wars, and he was now so powerful that he had become known as "Puffy" in New York City's Prince Street's Black community.

The Rap Mogul Sean "Puffy" Combs and his "Baby Mother," Kimberly Porter, were arrested and charged with drug trafficking. This article investigates and argues that their arrests were part of an F.B.I. plan to use aspects of the drug trade to monitor, guide, and control the inner workings of the darkest corners of the entertainment industry. Viewed solely in terms of legal and moral consequences, the federal law enforcement reasoning behind selecting them and hoping to make their arrests stick can be justified. Evaluated from the perspective of the realpolitik of the F.B.I., Combs and Porter constituted win-win targets. On one hand, the law enforcers hoped to turn Blow Up into a second Serpico and, by spooking these other famous Black people, blacken them further. Moreover, the same tactics proved helpful in controlling and corrupt them with a wish to have following services with the musicians' and entertainers' inner workings ever since Woodstock attracted close federal scrutiny to the activities of what the F.B.I.'s leader then, J. Edgar Hoover, had vehemently assured President R. Nixon constituted the 'nihilistic and anarchist White Boys' from within whose ranks and according to an F.B.I. analysis were sufficient numbers of drug making and distributing agitators.

Diddy continued to produce hits, and his on-the-spot talent led Interscope founder Jimmy Lovine to release the promising rapper Eminem. After convincing Eminem that he was a rap guru during a digic meeting, Diddy introduced Tom-what to his newfound starving friend, Dr. Dre. Despite running a successful indicative quotid in the late 1990s, Diddy's bad luck * * continued. In 1999, Diddy was acquitted of spotty, gun-taught, paved beats that led to strange shirts ($ 17,000) in connection with a stampede at one of its guts. Diddy was lucky; the unfortunate, the victims of the murder *... were not so fortunate. Of course, Diddy had great success in the 2000s, releasing two titles for "No Way Out" alongside his free troll and reuniting with Dr. Dre and Eminem after selling 2 million copies of "Heal Wig?!. ?," the first release of "Forever." His only setback in the 2000s was his protege G.D.M.,* who made anti-homophobic slurs under extreme public pressure*. Combs, who founded

BAD BOYS records, was a military psychologist who found victims in 2007* from a murder aboard a boat P.I.R. the "I am on a boat," P.I.R. the "I am on a boat" P. Diddy was arrested in Los Angeles for raping his former model one night after his birthday, Cassandra Kenny.

P. Diddy, born al Sean Combs, took the rap world by storm by being arguably the most prominent record executive in the history of the genre, as Diddy managed, co-produced, or had the idea for some of the biggest releases of the genre, including "Jump," the first release from no-tro-rappers Krys Kross, Biggie's "Ready to Die" album Public's "No Way Out," Mase's "Harlem World" and "No way out for Nas. Diddy, a close associate of the late Aaliyah, also produces R&B hits and dabbles on the front end. Born in New York City on November 4, 1969, Diddy has a colorful and tragic life. Diddy, left orphaned at age two, received a full-time athletic training scholarship at Howard University thanks to his wealthy ex-wife. Diddy expelled Griffeth from his class in 1991 after learning that the cops were looking for him. Griffeth then went to an audition for "Uptown Records," where he got an internship. Griffith later received a record contract and became a successful rapper named Big Williams. Diddy fearlessly threatened Malicious Griffeth, ensuring that there was a rift in Hip-Hop between the two rappers. In 1993, Diddy was arrested for attacking ground-lover Jerami Strong. As a result of the attack, Strong went blind. Diddy was spared serious charges in Kase's lawsuit * *, but he ended up with probation.

Accusations of trafficking involving P. Diddy surfaced amidst a climate of heightened scrutiny over the treatment of artists and industry practices. Reports suggested that P. Diddy was involved in exploiting aspiring musicians, coercing them into unfair contracts, and profiting off their talents without adequate compensation. These allegations struck at the heart of the music industry's power dynamics and raised concerns about exploitation and abuse within the entertainment world.

The allegations against P. Diddy must be understood within the broader context of the music industry's history of exploitation and manipulation. For decades, artists, particularly those from marginalized backgrounds, have faced systemic barriers to success, often at the hands of influential industry figures. P. Diddy's rise to prominence in the highly competitive hip-hop world further fueled speculation about his methods and motivations.

While allegations against P. Diddy have circulated in the media and among industry insiders, concrete evidence of trafficking remains elusive. Investigations into his business practices and dealings with artists have yielded mixed results, with some suggesting patterns of exploitation and others finding no conclusive evidence of wrongdoing. The music industry's lack of transparency and accountability complicates efforts to uncover the truth behind the allegations.

The allegations against P. Diddy have had far-reaching implications for the music industry, casting a shadow over the reputations of artists and industry insiders alike. The controversy has sparked conversations about power dynamics, accountability, and ethical conduct in entertainment. It has also highlighted the need for greater protections for artists and stricter regulations to prevent exploitation and abuse.

The allegations of trafficking involving P. Diddy underscore the challenges of confronting exploitation and abuse in the music industry. While the truth behind the accusations remains uncertain, the controversy has sparked meaningful discussions about accountability and justice. Moving forward, the music industry must prioritize transparency, fairness, and the well-being of artists to ensure a more equitable and ethical landscape for all involved.

So Diddy's claims fall squarely into Kit Bitshiver's category of large public claims with dangerous admissions but small public claims likely to infringe copyright law. The danger of being the target of an RICO investigation is a tangible consequence of not admitting to the full extent of one's prior involvement in a particular line of broken laws. But as the Post indicates, merely walking into a crackhouse or conducting a drug operation on a scale so small as not to be described as a large-scale trafficking operation does not sound as bad. Diddy possibly was not in much danger of infringing the default civil standard of $750 worth of damage for each sound recording infringed earlier; he almost certainly is not in danger of severe repercussions for his claims of a mid-level role in an operation smaller than those described in court papers recently.

P. Diddy's recent claims in an HBO interview about being involved in a crack operation in the mid-80s have been reported and not sensationalized. Despite the New York Post's report that prominently conveys the impression that Diddy admitted to heading up a drug operation on such a large scale that he was comfortable inside the crack house with the money, the interviewer softens the claim a bit in the actual story, noting that Diddy smiles and says, "You trying to get me locked up... I wasn't the one in a crack house with a gun." But the Post seems to conflate walking into a crackhouse unarmed and conducting a more significant scale trafficking operation. Apologist Agent notes today, "Even at its most literal, where Diddy was selling stuff, nearly a ton of stuff was seized in a single raid yesterday."

Recognizing and Addressing Human Trafficking in the United States of America

In the labyrinth of contemporary society, where innocence should be cherished and protected, there exists a harrowing reality: human trafficking. As guardians of our children's well-being, it falls upon us to remain vigilant to the subtle cues that may signal their vulnerability to trafficking. This chapter delves into the critical insights gained from conversations with David, shedding light on the multifaceted nature of human trafficking and the imperative for collective action in combating this pervasive crime.

Human trafficking stands as a modern-day form of slavery, preying upon the vulnerable and exploiting their most basic rights and dignity. David and I embarked on a journey to unravel its complexities, emphasizing its definition as the recruitment, transportation, harboring, or exploitation of individuals through coercion, deception, or force for forced labor or commercial sexual exploitation. We recognized its diverse forms, from labor trafficking in various industries to commercial sexual exploitation targeting women and children.

As parents, we emphasized the importance of vigilance in recognizing the signs of human trafficking, especially among vulnerable populations like children, immigrants, and those facing economic hardship. David and I discussed key indicators of trafficking, including changes in behavior, unexplained possessions, secrecy about activities, and sudden influxes of resources. We underscored the significance of monitoring children's online activities, as traffickers often exploit online platforms for recruitment and grooming.

Human trafficking education emerged as a critical component in our discussions. We emphasized the importance of equipping ourselves and our children with the knowledge necessary to recognize the signs of trafficking and navigate the world safely. By teaching children about the strategies used by traffickers and fostering open communication within families, we empower them to make informed decisions and seek guidance when needed. Furthermore, we highlighted the role of community collaboration in raising awareness and fostering a united front against exploitation.

In the face of the human trafficking crisis, reporting suspected cases emerged as a moral imperative. David and I stressed the importance of documenting observations, providing detailed information to law enforcement agencies, and cooperating fully with investigations. We emphasized the need for swift and decisive action to protect victims and hold perpetrators accountable, urging communities to get involved and support law enforcement efforts.

In conclusion, our conversations underscored the urgent need for collective action to combat human trafficking. David and I affirmed our commitment to raising awareness, enhancing victim support services, and addressing root causes of vulnerability. We emphasized the importance of community engagement and urged individuals to become advocates for change. By prioritizing human trafficking education within our families and communities, we can create a safer and more resilient future for our children. Let us stand united in our commitment to protect the vulnerable and build a future free from exploitation, one conversation at a time.

Supporting Human Trafficking Victims and Preventing Exploitation Through Community Action in the darkness of human trafficking, survivors often find themselves trapped in a nightmare of exploitation and abuse. Yet, amidst the shadows, there is a glimmer of hope—a network of support services and compassionate allies dedicated to helping survivors reclaim their lives and rebuild their futures. This chapter explores the journey of healing and recovery for human trafficking victims and outlines key strategies for preventing exploitation through community awareness and action.

Supporting Human Trafficking Victims for those who have endured the horrors of human trafficking, the road to recovery may seem daunting. However, they are not alone. A range of support services stands ready to offer compassion, guidance, and resources to survivors as they navigate the journey towards healing and empowerment. From shelters and safe houses providing immediate safety and refuge to counseling and therapy services offering specialized support for trauma recovery, survivors have access to a network of care tailored to their unique needs. Legal assistance services ensure that survivors' rights are protected, while medical care addresses their physical and mental health needs. Nonprofit organizations dedicated to combating human trafficking provide advocacy, case management, and education, empowering survivors to rebuild their lives with dignity and resilience.

In the battle against human trafficking, parents serve as frontline defenders, equipped with the power of knowledge, vigilance, and proactive engagement. By educating themselves about the tactics and signs of trafficking, parents can recognize and respond to potential threats, safeguarding their children from exploitation. Cultivating open communication within families creates a safe space for children to seek guidance and share their experiences, while monitoring online activities helps parents protect their children from digital risks. Empowering children with knowledge about trafficking tactics and building their resilience equips them to navigate the world safely. Community engagement plays a crucial role in preventing exploitation, with law enforcement agencies, advocacy groups, and other stakeholders working together to raise awareness and support survivors. By fostering a culture of vigilance, compassion, and action, communities can create a protective shield around vulnerable individuals, ensuring a future free from exploitation.

Human trafficking by gangs poses a complex and far-reaching threat to communities across the United States. By infiltrating neighborhoods, exploiting vulnerable youth, and perpetuating fear and control, these criminal enterprises perpetuate cycles of exploitation and oppression. Law enforcement agencies, community organizations, and stakeholders must work together to disrupt gang-related trafficking networks, rescue victims, and hold perpetrators accountable.

Multidisciplinary task forces, public awareness campaigns, and targeted interventions are essential components of a comprehensive response to gang-involved trafficking. By addressing root causes, supporting victims, and strengthening law enforcement efforts, communities can dismantle the grip of gangs and offer hope to those trapped in exploitation.

In the fight against human trafficking, healing and prevention are intertwined, rooted in compassion, resilience, and collective action. By supporting survivors on their journey to healing and empowering communities to prevent exploitation, we can create a future where every individual is free to live with dignity and freedom. Together, let us stand united in our commitment to combatting human trafficking, offering healing and hope to all those affected by this insidious crime.

A Comprehensive Approach to Combat Human Trafficking is a grave violation of human rights, perpetuating exploitation and suffering on a global scale. This chapter explores critical strategies for combating human trafficking, encompassing legal frameworks, law enforcement responses, victim support services, and prevention efforts. By implementing a comprehensive approach, stakeholders can work towards eradicating trafficking and safeguarding the rights and dignity of survivors.

Human trafficking encompasses a range of exploitative practices, including forced labor, sex trafficking, and organ trafficking. It thrives in various settings, fueled by factors such as poverty, inequality, conflict, and limited opportunities. Victims endure physical and psychological trauma, perpetuating cycles of poverty and sustaining organized crime networks. Recognizing the silent cries of trafficking victims is essential in breaking the cycle of indifference and advocating for change.

Trafficking victims endure profound suffering and trauma, including psychological, emotional, and physical abuse. They grapple with depression, anxiety, PTSD, and complex trauma, enduring violence, torture, and degradation at the hands of their traffickers. Survivor testimonies provide invaluable insights into the hidden realities of trafficking, shedding light on the insidious tactics employed by traffickers and the daunting challenges faced in seeking justice and recovery.

Traffickers exploit vulnerabilities for financial gain, ranging from organized crime syndicates to individual perpetrators and corrupt officials. Demand fuels the market for trafficking, perpetuated by sex buyers and exploitative employers. Weak legal frameworks, corruption, and societal norms normalize exploitation and hinder prosecution efforts. Addressing corruption within law enforcement agencies is crucial for combating trafficking effectively and ensuring accountability.

International legal frameworks and conventions provide essential tools for combating trafficking and holding perpetrators accountable. Law enforcement agencies play a crucial role in investigating trafficking, rescuing victims, and dismantling trafficking networks. Victim support and rehabilitation services are essential for survivors' recovery journey, encompassing shelters, counseling, medical care, legal assistance, and reintegration programs. Prevention efforts target root causes and vulnerability among at-risk populations through education, awareness campaigns, and economic empowerment initiatives.

Combating human trafficking requires a multifaceted approach that addresses legal, law enforcement, victim support, and prevention aspects. By implementing comprehensive strategies and fostering collaboration among stakeholders, we can work towards eradicating trafficking, protecting survivors, and creating a safer and more just world for all.

Understanding and Confronting Family Trafficking

Family trafficking lurks within the shadows of our society, manifesting in the most intimate of relationships where trust should abound. Unlike conventional trafficking narratives, family trafficking ensnares its victims within the confines of their own homes, perpetuating cycles of exploitation and abuse across generations. This chapter endeavors to unravel the complexities of family trafficking, delving into its definitions, causes, manifestations, and the intricate web of legal, social, and cultural challenges that obstruct effective intervention. By shedding light on this clandestine form of exploitation, we aim to catalyze comprehensive strategies to combat family trafficking and safeguard the sanctity of familial relationships.

Family trafficking transcends the conventional understanding of trafficking, infiltrating the heart of familial relationships. Perpetrated not by external actors, but by caregivers and relatives entrusted with protection, family trafficking blurs the boundaries between safety and exploitation. Its systemic nature perpetuates intergenerational cycles of abuse, embedding trauma and victimization deep within family dynamics. Victims, ensnared by complex power dynamics and cultural norms, often find themselves trapped in a web of silence and complicity, further complicating efforts to seek help and break free from their abusers.

The genesis of family trafficking lies in a nexus of social, economic, and cultural factors that fuel vulnerability and exploitation within families. Economic hardship amplifies susceptibility to exploitation, as perpetrators exploit financial desperation to coerce victims into labor or sexual servitude. Cultural beliefs and gender norms perpetuate power imbalances, fostering environments where abuse thrives under the guise of tradition. Substance abuse and mental health disorders exacerbate vulnerabilities, rendering victims more susceptible to manipulation and control.

Despite international commitments to combat human trafficking, legal and political barriers impede effective intervention against family trafficking. Gaps in legal frameworks, coupled with challenges in victim identification and prosecution, hinder justice for victims and accountability for perpetrators. The hidden nature of family trafficking complicates efforts to detect and address exploitation within familial relationships, necessitating comprehensive strategies that prioritize victim rights and cross-border cooperation.

Confronting family trafficking demands a multifaceted approach, uniting law enforcement, judicial systems, and social services in a coordinated effort. Law enforcement agencies must diligently investigate cases, dismantle trafficking networks, and rescue victims from exploitative situations. Judicial systems play a pivotal role in prosecuting traffickers and providing legal remedies to victims, ensuring their rights and needs are upheld throughout legal proceedings. Social service agencies offer essential support and assistance to empower victims on their journey towards healing and independence.

Family trafficking thrives in the shadows of our society, perpetuating cycles of exploitation and abuse within the supposed sanctity of familial relationships. By unraveling its complexities and confronting the challenges it poses, we can forge a path towards justice, healing, and resilience for victims of family trafficking. Through collective action and unwavering commitment, we can dismantle the chains of exploitation and safeguard the fundamental rights and dignity of every individual, within and beyond the confines of the family unit.

Unveiling the Plight of Family Trafficking with Family trafficking, veiled within the sanctity of familial bonds, imposes harrowing exploitation and abuse upon its victims. This chapter serves as a beacon, illuminating the multifaceted dimensions of family trafficking and advocating for holistic responses to prevent, intervene, and rehabilitate. Non-governmental organizations (NGOs) and governmental agencies stand as pillars in this endeavor, providing frontline assistance, advocating for policy reform, and fostering collaboration to combat family trafficking.

NGOs, with their specialized expertise and unwavering dedication, serve as lifelines for victims of family trafficking. Through victim identification, trauma-informed care, and social support services, NGOs offer essential assistance and advocacy, ensuring victims receive the care and attention they deserve. Meanwhile, governmental agencies at all levels play pivotal roles in policy development, implementation, and coordination. Inter-agency collaboration fosters a cohesive response, enhancing victim support, and strengthening anti-trafficking efforts.

Victims of family trafficking require immediate and comprehensive support to escape their exploitative situations and begin their journey towards recovery. Safe and secure shelter provides a refuge from abuse, while access to medical care addresses physical and mental health needs resulting from exploitation. Legal assistance empowers victims to navigate legal proceedings and seek justice, ensuring their rights are upheld throughout the process.

Empowering victims through education, vocational training, and job opportunities fosters economic independence and reduces vulnerability to re-exploitation. Psychosocial support and counseling services offer avenues for healing and resilience, helping victims rebuild their lives in the aftermath of trauma. Social integration and community support promote a sense of belonging and inclusion, empowering survivors to reclaim their agency and advocate for their rights.

Initiatives such as the Philippine Inter-Agency Council Against Trafficking (IACAT) demonstrate the power of inter-agency collaboration in combating trafficking and protecting victims. Adopting a victim-centered approach, the Philippines prioritizes victim support and public awareness, fostering a national response to trafficking. Similarly, the Swedish Model targets the demand for commercial sex, providing comprehensive support services to victims and individuals in prostitution, while advocating for policy reform and international cooperation.

Family trafficking remains a pervasive and insidious threat, necessitating concerted efforts from all stakeholders to combat exploitation and protect the rights of victims. By prioritizing victim support, enhancing legal frameworks, and fostering collaboration among governments, NGOs, and civil society, we can illuminate paths towards a future free from family trafficking. Together, let us stand as beacons of hope, guiding survivors towards healing, recovery, and empowerment.

Understanding and Addressing Human Trafficking to be a sinister global phenomenon thriving in the shadows, preys upon the vulnerable, stripping them of freedom and dignity. Despite widespread acknowledgment of its enormity, solutions remain elusive. The burden to combat this scourge falls upon society as a whole, necessitating collective action.

Reflecting on the dire state of human trafficking underscores the imperative for comprehensive training programs, equipping law enforcement to combat this injustice effectively. Addressing the demand for exploitative services, particularly in the commercial sex industry, is paramount. Education and measures like trafficking-free zones disrupt profitability and diminish traffickers' incentives. The disproportionate impact on women and children is deeply troubling. Despite reports indicating widespread exploitation, only a fraction of cases are reported. The case study of Birmingham, Alabama, illustrates the prevalence of trafficking even within our communities, necessitating specialized interventions and support services. combating human trafficking demands unwavering commitment and collective action. It calls for challenging societal norms, advocating for policy reforms, and providing support to survivors, envisioning a world where exploitation and trafficking are intolerable.

Confronting the Epidemic
of Missing and Murdered
Indigenous Women

The relentless epidemic of missing and murdered Indigenous women in the United States stands as an urgent humanitarian crisis demanding immediate and concerted action. This chapter delves into the alarming statistics surrounding missing and murdered Indigenous women, scrutinizes the systemic failures within law enforcement and community responses, and underscores the dire need for equitable treatment and justice for Indigenous women. Through poignant documentaries such as "If I Go Missing," "Bring Her Home," and "Missing From Fire Trail Road," we amplify the voices of Indigenous women, illuminating their resilience and defiance in the face of pervasive injustice.

Indigenous communities across the United States bear an unjust burden with disproportionately high rates of missing and murdered women, laying bare a systemic failure to safeguard and uphold their rights. This crisis starkly underscores the intersecting layers of gender-based violence, racial discrimination, and the enduring trauma inflicted upon Indigenous peoples throughout history.

Regrettably, both law enforcement agencies and communities frequently fall short in their responses to reports of missing Indigenous women, perpetuating a cycle of neglect and impunity. Stereotypes, biases, and entrenched institutional barriers contribute to the chronic underreporting and mishandling of cases, further marginalizing Indigenous victims and their grieving families.

Indigenous women unequivocally deserve equal treatment and protection under the law, yet they continue to endure discrimination and indifference in their pursuit of justice. It is imperative to challenge and dismantle these stereotypes and biases to redress systemic injustices and ensure that Indigenous women receive the same level of attention and support as other victims of crime.

The impact of documentaries like "If I Go Missing" cannot be overstated—they serve as potent catalysts for advocacy and awareness, empowering Indigenous communities to demand justice and accountability for their missing loved ones. By amplifying the voices of Indigenous women and shedding light on their harrowing experiences, these documentaries mobilize support and solidarity in the fight against violence and injustice.

Similarly, "Bring Her Home" poignantly illustrates the resilience and defiance of Indigenous women who refuse to remain silent in the face of injustice. Through their unwavering advocacy for their missing relatives and impassioned calls for systemic change, these women inspire courage and solidarity, challenging societal norms and galvanizing collective action to address the root causes of violence and discrimination.

"Missing From Fire Trail Road" lays bare the grim realities of crimes perpetrated against Indigenous women, laying bare the systemic failures and institutional neglect perpetuating the epidemic of missing and murdered Indigenous women. This documentary serves as a sobering wake-up call, compelling policymakers, law enforcement agencies, and communities to take substantive action to confront the underlying causes of violence and ensure justice for missing Indigenous women.

Through tireless advocacy, heightened awareness, and unified collective action, we can endeavor to halt the epidemic of missing and murdered Indigenous women, ensuring that each woman is not only valued and protected but also remembered. By confronting systemic failures head-on and amplifying the voices of Indigenous women, we can forge a more just and equitable society—one where every individual is treated with the dignity, respect, and compassion they unequivocally deserve.

The highest risk is consequent is isolation in relationships with Indigenous men because offenders engage in and rely on victim-blaming genderized racism and colonial disrespect. Once a firm belief in otherness has been achieved, other harmful responses become more acceptable, such as Indigenous women as consumable objects and instruments of the offender's desires. Deviant distinctions increase the number of missing and murdered Indigenous women. Offenders are encouraged and willing to try new methods of isolation. As Indigenous women lack free will, offenders can focus on pushing boundaries with victims, which is necessary to achieve confidence in a particular tactic. Genderized racism meant Indigenous women were always non-deserving victims. Given Indigenous people were, in the offender's perspective and eye, undeserving of societal protection, it became increasingly more challenging for stakeholders to moderate and mitigate potential shields.

A report on missing and murdered Indigenous women. It is outrageous that in 2021, there is not enough data or resources to determine the scope of this criminal violence. This epidemic of violence must end, and the victims must be remembered. A problem in itself is the ignorance surrounding the pandemic of murdered and missing Indigenous women. Historical and contemporary violence has led to the implementation of a genocidal infrastructure denying the existence and value of Indigenous women. For many, these women are not accurate and complete human beings but rather disposable commodities to exploit, purchase, and murder. It is the failure to see Indigenous women as human beings of dignity and respect and the willingness to exploit them as sex objects that leads to the epidemic of missing and murdered Indigenous women.

NVIC has begun a campaign to help federal, state, local, and tribal governments eliminate this disparity in response to Indian women's suffering. Such solutions as enhanced communication about investigations, additional coordination between authorities on missing and murdered cases, and the need to address perceptions about missing and murdered Indian women require political and legal discourse. The U.S. Senate held a hearing on November 22 to address the legislative changes necessary to address the issue. Concerns include the need for government-wide consultation and an enhanced law enforcement presence. The hearing focused on S. 1942, the Not Invisible Act, designed to address the many problems in the administration of justice that affect the outcomes of criminal cases.

There are several legal and cultural obstacles related to the pandemic of murdered and missing indigenous women in Indian Country. Cultural obstacles include:

+ The public's, law enforcement's, and courts' prejudice toward indigenous women.
+ There is a lack of communication and collaboration regarding investigations.
+ The mistrust that victims' families have for tribe, state, and federal institutions.

Legal challenges include the gaps that prohibit tribal authorities from prosecuting non-Indian perpetrators and the lack of coordination among law enforcement and across sovereign jurisdictions. These challenges are compounded by logistics, workforce, and the lack of resources for underpaid and overworked law enforcement agents.

The lasting influence of these schools generated a form of culture shock within the Indian community and propagated severe intergenerational and transgenerational child abuse (i.e., immediate family members were subsequent victims/multi-stressed abusers). This chaos created many native children/families having contact with various child and family services (CFS) systems, further resulting in many children being taken from their families. Residential schools experienced significant obstacles in creating systematic behavior change in the generations of indigenous people. They impacted and entreated indigenous people into a state of socio-economic and political oppression.

Hundreds of years ago, substantial disparities in power, economic opportunities, and resources between American settlers and indigenous populations generated a push to diminish the cultural autonomy of these populations from American settler society. Significant efforts to aggressively impose classical education on native people resulted in large numbers of American Indian children being placed in churches and mission-run public schools where they were severely punished if they communicated in their native tongues. The extensive time native children spent in these schools separated them from their families and tribes. When they ultimately received permission to return home, the negative behaviors they learned made re-assimilation especially difficult. The severe punishment they endured for speaking their native languages led to many losing fluency in their home language and resulted in them being ostracized from native society and incapable of participating in American culture because of their Indian heritage.

This situation requires a swift response to restore a sense of safety to our families and communities. The difficult task of actively addressing the epidemic of murdered and missing American Indians and Alaska Natives falls on the Operation Lady Justice Task Force. Our Task Force is working to bring the entire arsenal of the Federal Government and its resources to bear on solving this issue and restoring our people's safety and security. In addition to protecting our people from the impacts of addiction and tribal criminality, U.S. Attorney Chris Myers called the short staffing of tribal law enforcement officers a significant challenge in addressing crime at reservations. The unique criminal jurisdictional issues also present unique challenges in investigating crimes involving missing and murdered Indigenous people.

According to studies done by the United Nations, in many cases, Indigenous identification disappears altogether because, in part, the deaths are categorized as multi-racial. Three studies in New Zealand by McCausland identified as part of Māori further into the study in the Appendices. The number of murders that are officially reported as murder and the number of homicides that are classed as such differ by a significant 8%, with a more considerable prevalence for victims who are Māori. In the same year, there were 22% more Māori victims identified in records of reportable offending in severe crimes, including murder and grievous bodily injury, than there were Māori females in the workforce (20%). These are significant elements." Atrociously high rates of homicide and missing persons are occurring among Native American and Alaskan women and girls. Both Alaska and India are experiencing crises. Too many families have loved ones gone missing.

The following data snapshots illustrate several essential points. First and foremost, data collection methodologies must be improved. There can be no justice for missing and murdered women without the ability to count and track these cases. The challenges are many. Second, the new data collection methodologies described illustrate that the epidemic of violence against indigenous women is worse than we ever believed. For example, in 2008, the Department of Justice reported that 2,389 American Indian and Alaska Native women were missing. The 2016 National Crime Information Center's report shed light on only 5,712 reports of missing American Indian and Alaska Native women and girls.

Further, those numbers jumped to 8,540 reports in 2017 and 10,656 reports in 2018. With these new and revised data collections relying on self-reported surveys, this can only be the tip of the iceberg. The data collections indicate that 94% of workplaces and 45% of NES workers surveyed reported that crimes against American Indians went unreported – often, these crimes were women who were missing or murdered.

The report presents historical and contemporary context, impacts on tribal nations and their women, legal reforms and recommendations, and tribal community issues and impacts. While the report contains numbers and statistics, it is important to remember that rather than being numbers, the research reveals the names and stories of those missing and murdered. These family members belonged to and were loved by their families and communities. Everyone feels their loss. They should never be forgotten. When reading the statistics, please remember that these numbers represent women and families impacted and shaped by a large discussion and necessary action for change.

The crisis is rooted in layers of blame and disconnect between the non-Indigenous and Indigenous communities, leaving Indigenous women in a highly vulnerable position. Fundamentally, colonialism ousted Indigenous matrilines from positions of authority, leading to inequity and violence among Indigenous women. Since the arrival of European settlers, Indigenous women have experienced increasing rates of violence and death, fostering cycles of persistent disparities and danger. Despite a rise in concern over the specific risks Indigenous women face, national and regional databases often omit essential information or contain errors, compounding revelations over the extent of this issue within Canada. Official data tends to be incomplete or contains faults. Yet, the fact that many Canadian Indigenous women are killed or go missing each year, disproportionate to their non-Indigenous counterparts, reinforces the need for national dialogue and attitudinal shifts to address these disparities. Furthermore, the historical stigmatization of Indigenous women within Canadian society has undermined efforts to address the situation.

It tackles the problem of murdered and missing Indigenous women. Not only is the epidemic of murdered and missing Indigenous women a long-standing social issue, but it is also a direct outcome of intricately linked systems of racial and gender-based oppression, racism's legacy, and colonialism that still permeate our institutions and public consciousness. A comprehensive examination of the MMIW phenomenon, starting with a description and definition of the pandemic and on to contributing variables and risk factors. This synopsis aids in defining and clarifying the consequences of a range of policies that either specifically aim to reduce the death toll or, paradoxically, are having an effect or may have an impact in the event of alternate adoption.

The Hearts report, as well as an earlier Portland, Oregon Report on the unfair treatment of Native Americans by local law enforcement (referred to throughout this report), echoes issues raised by families and community members. According to an Indigenous woman who attended a missing clinic session sponsored by the Wisconsin DOJ, knowledgeable about communication issues with tribes, we are not always informed when there are missing individuals as a result of a policy that permits discrimination based on race. Race affects the level of law enforcement response. A recent Portland, Oregon report found law enforcement is deeply involved in not responding to crimes against Native Americans in some jurisdictions.

- Officers not adequately trained in cultural and historical sensitivities. - They did not have a good grasp of tribal jurisdiction. - They were poorly paid and had high turnover rates. - Little or no understanding of the MMIW issue and the extent of it. - Police lack interest in

MMIW. - Family members of missing and murdered Indigenous women accused officers of lacking interest and following up when women, girls, or two-spirit individuals went missing.

The fundamental issue that joins these criminal justice failures is systemic racism and discrimination. The failure of law enforcement to respond to these cases as they would to the disappearance of a young non-Indian woman is quite simply a devaluing of American Indian women. The Hearts of Our People report, issued by the Minnesota Indian Women's Resource Center, found that law enforcement officers are deeply involved in violence against Native peoples.

Federal law enforcement has limited resources, especially in rural areas. Many law enforcement agencies fight against drug or drug-related offenses, and a significant workload is associated with federal land management in a growing number of police agencies. Agencies that initiate tribal law have high levels of responsibilities, but only for Native American reservations, and may be overworked, situated far away, or unrecognizable with appropriate resolutions. In addition, very few votes – less than 47% of Native lands – are under federal control while coercing the federal government to monitor extensive Native lands. Finally, the adoption of Native women intensified the negative correlations between females and European colonizers with displacement. It forced assimilation, which led to the still constant exploitation of sexual violence and elimination of Natives as opposed to the exploitation of assault and displacement.

Data on missing and murdered Native women is disturbing and neglected. Little comprehensive data exists. However, the National Crime Information Center reported that in 2016, 5,712 reports of missing American Indian and Alaska Native females were made. Only 116 were logged in the U.S. Department of Justice Database. Many Native women have experienced violence from a romantic or sexual partner at a significant number. The data is frightening but often inadequate. Lack of investigation and condoning of these crimes allows perpetrators to act with impunity. Some believe that the most common characteristic of crime is the absence of proper investigation: to align police, including those from different police departments, and health issues, as well as ways to determine the circumstances under which violent deaths occur. The families searched for missing Native women and engaged in acts of desperation. When there is a weak industrial police force and fragile funding, an excessive load is being placed.

We believe that the complexity of the legal and jurisdictional environments of Indian Country has made it difficult for off-reservation police departments to engage in the nuanced learning about the unique commitment and trust responsibilities owed by federal and Indian and native rights and interests that the federal government has historically established. More education, training, and experience in dealing with murder and missing indigenous women cases would enhance cooperation. Other improvements, such as increased use of tribal liaison officers, could alleviate the jurisdictional sharing problems and also improve the relationships between some off-reservation PDs and their local tribes. More active and effective tribal police might also help to ease some off-reservation PDs out of the entrenched views that tribal PDs and the reservation communities they serve are not capable of effectively dealing with MMW cases. Similarly, better integration and utilization of tribally-specific contextual education can be shaped generally to improve off-reservation treatment of the tribal communities they serve.

Across Indian Country, effective responses to MMW are hampered by the complicated legal and jurisdictional environments within which the problem is situated. Federal and state complicated jurisdictional agreements are made out of context, with the real-life situations that reservation populations experience being solely delegatory. The practical implications of the complex legal bases for jurisdiction in Indian Country are often neglected. Jurisdictional conflicts and the allocation of judicial authority in cases involving Indians are not limited to Indian Country, but the complexities and resulting uncertainties are most evident.

Studies show that for every five jobs created in another industry in a Native American community, at least one of these jobs will be made in Indian-owned businesses. The longer we wait to reduce violence against American Indian and Alaska Native women by strengthening their tribal justice systems, the harder it will be to grow the economy. We must address this challenge limiting the security of all American families. It is disgraceful that any Member of Congress would offer up proposals to eliminate all of the critical elements for continuing the success of VAWA—tangible and sustainable results and a demonstrated commitment to ending violence against women on tribal lands. Duro should be overturned so that tribal nations have control over their own criminal and civil jurisdiction.

Legal accountability for such cruel behavior is of vital importance. Let me share with you an alarming statistic: approximately 34% of American Indian and Alaska Native women will be raped. When the rape victim is an American Indian or Alaska Native woman, the perpetrator can evade justice simply by being a non-Indian man. The Justice Department has correctly recognized that on reservations, there is a higher rate of sexual violence and that the majority of the perpetrators are non-Indian. However, when there is no legal deterrent, that means that rape is effectively a tool for those who want to harm Native women. Consequently, the lack of legal protection and the cycle of trauma continue and are demonstrated by the fact that American Indian and Alaska Native women are 2.5 times more likely to experience sexual assault from a perpetrator who is not an Indian.

The disproportionate institutional response to crime also reflects broader structural problems that have historically marginalized American Indians. This marginalization has led to, at least partially, an ongoing disregard for the safety of Native women. Throughout colonization, American Indian women have been deemed "less" by ideals of European womanhood and resulting dual citizenship systems as opposites that reinforce stereotypes at either end. Colonization has also resulted in higher rates of poverty and poor access to healthcare, the leading healthcare-related factors for both the COVID-19 and MMIW crises. Further, since their inception, the federal and pre-state penal systems and their employees have often treated criminals as mere caretakers for an inferior racially inferior population.

More general awareness and advocacy are steps in the right direction, but many advocates stress that education within and about the politically insular world of tribal nations is crucial. More robust support from Montana's Attorney General, direction from a Governor-appointed advisory council and other political leaders, and guidance and resources to develop self-directed economic development centered on reservation needs are but a few solutions emerging from the 1.5% Indian coalition. Without tribal awareness and local dialogue about these often-horrifying crimes, criminal offenders float through even the closest-knit communities, perpetrating acts of violence for decades without fear of consequences.

The reauthorization in 2018 of VAWA reflects the legislation's expansion in service access for indigenous women who have been victimized, and it recognizes the inherent sovereignty of tribal communities. For the first time, the 2013 reauthorization of VAWA recognized tribes' jurisdiction over non-indigenous people, all of which can safely and effectively bring VAWA to justice.

However, for non-indigenous offenders, this jurisdictional expansion faces numerous legal loopholes. Since its implementation, the 2018 VAWA reauthorization has allowed for the direct prosecution of non-Indian perpetrators. While VAWA's inherent sovereignty expansion for native women and their communities has gained widespread support and recognition, VAWA's failure to extend concurrent criminal jurisdiction over non-indigenous offenders has created jurisdictional disparities, more gaps in public safety, and increased anxiety for Indian women. VAWA's attempt to provide tribal authorities with the needed authority to protect their communities, including measures in place since the expiration of VAWA's program permits, such as the Addington Criminal Offenses Act, to help push the Mukasey amendments into law. Alongside positive changes in funding, more programs and local law enforcement agencies have received essential training to recognize domestic violence and cultural competency. They should continue, both of which are crucial components of the tribal criminal justice systems, as they work towards objectives that lead to the prevention of violence for their community members. Upon VAWA reauthorizations in 2013 and 2018, legislative reforms have significantly expanded future law enforcement protections for Native American and Alaskan Native communities and have the potential to save countless lives from the brutal violence associated with contemporary missing and murdered indigenous women.

The criminal justice system consistently fails to protect indigenous women, who are often marginalized in society. In response to the MMIW crisis, activists and lawmakers have worked toward legal reforms, including the reauthorization of the Violence Against Women Act in 2018. Legislative reform is only one potential solution to this problem. Social inequality, historical dispossession of land and wealth, and negative stereotypes and misperceptions all contribute to violence against native women. Despite legal reforms and increasing public awareness, the problem continues to escalate. As both a short-term and long-term solution, scholars suggest a systems-based approach that addresses the missing and murdered indigenous women's issue on multiple levels through community activism, policy implementation and analysis, and social changes. Any solutions to this crisis ought, to begin with recognizing how stereotypes of indigenous women contribute to violence against women - on the part of both native and non-native people - persist in society, the criminal justice system's failure to recognize indigenous women's right to protection, and a police force that often views these women as less valuable than "desirable victims". Policymakers, activists, and the public should work together to challenge these negative images that perpetuate violence and prevent justice for these victims and their families.

Community empowerment and healing. Indigenous peoples' justice efforts and call to action cross-national/tribal boundaries to address root causes of violence while enhancing community protective factors that promote strength, healing, and action-based change. The common crimes of femicide that are committed against Indigenous women, girls, and two-spirit individuals are part of the direct consequences of ongoing histories of colonialism and structures of oppression.

Allegations of Satanic Rituals and Pedophilia in Hollywood

We have long known that Satanists and pedophiles run the globe. Hollywood has long been portrayed as a beautiful world of fame and money, but the glittering surface conceals a darker reality. These insights, as well as the critical need for change awareness and activism, are examined.

Discussing allegations of Satanism and pedophilia in Hollywood requires careful consideration. While there have been claims and accusations, it's crucial to approach these topics with skepticism and rely on verifiable evidence rather than unsubstantiated rumors. However, I can provide an overview of the history of such allegations and the challenges in verifying them.

When discussing Satanism's influence on Hollywood, it's important to distinguish between the portrayal of Satanism in films and television shows and allegations of actual Satanic practices within the entertainment industry. While depictions of Satanic themes are common in popular culture, claims of real-life Satanic influence in Hollywood remain largely unsubstantiated. However, examining how Satanism is depicted in the media can provide insight into its cultural impact and influence.

The glitz and glamour of Hollywood have long been accompanied by whispers of darker, more sinister practices lurking beneath the surface. Among the most persistent rumors are allegations of Satanic rituals and pedophilia, casting a pall over the entertainment industry and fueling public concern. In this paper, we embark on a journey through the tangled history of these accusations, navigating the complexities of verification, and examining the profound legal and social implications they entail.

The origins of allegations regarding Satanic rituals and practices in Hollywood can be traced back decades, entwined with the sensationalized media reports and moral panic that characterized the notorious Satanic Panic of the 1980s. While many of these claims have since been debunked or proven unfounded, the specter of Satanic influence continues to loom large, with Hollywood often serving as the epicenter of suspicion.

Concurrently, the industry has grappled with a separate but equally troubling issue: the persistent concern over child exploitation and sexual abuse. High-profile scandals involving prominent figures such as Roman Polanski, Harvey Weinstein, and Jeffrey Epstein have thrust the issue into the spotlight, highlighting the prevalence of predatory behavior within the entertainment world.

Yet, verifying allegations of Satanic rituals and pedophilia in Hollywood is a formidable challenge, hampered by the elusive nature of concrete evidence. While isolated incidents may result in arrests or legal proceedings, proving the existence of widespread conspiracies remains elusive without verifiable proof, leaving many claims mired in ambiguity and uncertainty.

Compounding the difficulty of discerning truth from fiction is the entertainment industry's propensity for gossip and sensationalism. Rumors and conspiracy theories can spread like wildfire, blurring the lines between fact and speculation, and impeding efforts to address genuine concerns in a meaningful and constructive manner.

Moreover, accusations of Satanic rituals and pedophilia carry profound legal and social repercussions. False allegations have the potential to irreparably damage reputations and livelihoods, while authentic cases of abuse demand meticulous investigation and diligent prosecution. Striking a delicate balance between the pursuit of justice and the preservation of the presumption of innocence is paramount, underscoring the importance of careful scrutiny and discernment in navigating such fraught terrain.

Ultimately, the allegations of Satanic rituals and pedophilia in Hollywood remain shrouded in ambiguity and uncertainty, underscoring the need for vigilance, transparency, and responsible reporting. While legitimate concerns about exploitation and abuse merit attention and action, sensationalism and rumor-mongering only serve to obscure genuine efforts to address systemic issues within the entertainment industry. Moving forward, a commitment to integrity, accountability, and empathy is essential in fostering a culture of safety and respect for all individuals within the entertainment community.

The narrative you've presented blends elements of historical fact with speculative fiction and conspiracy theories. While Hollywood has indeed been associated with various religious and spiritual movements over the years, including some fringe groups, the claim about Satanism being worshipped in Hollywood since 1928 is not supported by credible evidence. Additionally, the mention of Maria Orsic and her supposed interactions with extraterrestrial beings in Antarctica appears to be a mix of historical inaccuracies and speculative storytelling.

It's important to critically evaluate information and discern fact from fiction, particularly when discussing sensitive topics like religion and the occult. While Hollywood has undoubtedly played a significant role in shaping cultural narratives and promoting certain ideologies, attributing the city's identity to Satanism and extraterrestrial encounters requires substantial evidence to support such claims.

If you're exploring themes related to religion, spirituality, or the influence of Hollywood on society, it may be more fruitful to focus on well-documented historical events and cultural phenomena rather than unsubstantiated rumors and conspiracy theories. This approach ensures a more grounded and intellectually honest discussion of the subject matter.

Hollywood's purported ties to Satanism often revolve around entertainment featuring themes of the Devil. One prominent example is the urban legend surrounding "Stairway to Heaven," a song by the British band Led Zeppelin. According to the legend, when played backward, the song allegedly contained a message inviting listeners to join the Church of Satan. Singer Robert Plant was rumored to have intentionally inserted covert and cryptic messages into the lyrics to pique interest in the song.

While this association between Hollywood and Satanism is largely rooted in urban folklore, it touches on significant aspects related to artistic freedom, albeit in exaggerated or insignificant ways. The notion of clandestine messages and hidden meanings in entertainment is not uncommon, often employed to provoke emotional responses or challenge societal norms. However, the truth behind such claims is often far more mundane than sensationalized rumors suggest.

Despite the prevalence of such myths, there have indeed been instances where Hollywood's portrayal of Satanism has had real-world consequences, albeit not necessarily detrimental to the Devil's image. Instances of controversial films or television shows depicting Satanic rituals or themes have occasionally sparked public outcry or religious condemnation. However, these instances are typically isolated and do not reflect a widespread endorsement of Satanism within the entertainment industry.

Moreover, it's essential to distinguish between artistic expression and genuine endorsement of Satanic beliefs. While Hollywood may explore provocative or taboo subjects for entertainment purposes, this does not equate to an endorsement of Satanism or an agenda to promote its ideals. Rather, it reflects the diverse and often provocative nature of artistic expression, which seeks to challenge, provoke, and entertain audiences.

while Hollywood's connection to Satanism may be perpetuated by myths and urban legends, the reality is far more nuanced. While instances of controversial content may stir controversy, they do not represent a concerted effort to promote or endorse Satanism. Instead, they reflect the complex interplay between artistic freedom, societal norms, and the quest for entertainment that characterizes the world of cinema.

In the twisted corridors of Hollywood's history, whispers of Satanic rituals and occult symbolism have woven themselves into the fabric of the entertainment industry's lore. From the mythic origins of Kenneth Anger's "Hollywood Babylon" to the enigmatic tales spun by BBC journalist Ben Thompson in "Ban This Filth! The Forbidden Pictures of Kenneth Anger," the shadowy underbelly of Tinseltown has long captivated the imagination of conspiracy theorists and skeptics alike.

One recurring motif in the narrative of Hollywood's alleged dalliance with Satanism is the infamous Bohemian Grove, a secluded retreat nestled among the redwoods of California. Here, titans of industry and politics purportedly convene for secretive gatherings shrouded in mystery and speculation. Accounts of unholy rituals and clandestine ceremonies have swirled around the grove for decades, with former U.S. Presidents and other influential figures lending credence to the rumors through their testimonies.

The murky nexus between power and the occult is further underscored by the symbolism and imagery that pervade Hollywood productions. From subtle nods to overt displays, Satanic motifs often find their way into films, television shows, and music videos, reflecting society's enduring fascination with the darker aspects of human nature. Whether it's the subtle incorporation of occult symbols or explicit references to Satanic rituals, these depictions serve to fascinate and provoke, tapping into primal fears and desires.

Yet, amidst the sensationalism and speculation, it's crucial to maintain a skeptical eye and separate fact from fiction. While allegations of Satanic influence in Hollywood may capture the public's imagination, verifiable evidence remains elusive. The line between artistic expression and genuine endorsement of Satanic beliefs is often blurred, further complicating efforts to discern the truth behind the glamour of Hollywood.

Ultimately, the allure of Hollywood's occult undercurrents continues to captivate and intrigue, inviting speculation and scrutiny in equal measure. We can navigate the tangled web of myth and reality that shrouds the entertainment industry's darkest secrets by approaching these allegations with critical inquiry and reliance on credible sources.

Christian Bale's Golden Globes acceptance speech in 2019, where he humorously thanked Satan for inspiring his portrayal of Dick Cheney, ignited discussions about Hollywood's alleged association with Luciferian practitioners. This paper delves into the controversy surrounding Bale's speech and examines broader themes of perceived

Luciferian influence within the entertainment industry. This research attempts to give a detailed picture of the relationship between popular culture and occult beliefs by examining conspiracy theories about Hollywood and evaluating responses from critics and Satanists.

Bale's humorous acknowledgment of Satan's purported influence during his acceptance speech at the 2019 Golden Globes, when he won Best Actor for his work in "Vice," was noteworthy. Despite being a jest, his remarks caused various emotions, from laughter to outrage. Even with its lighthearted tone, Bale's speech spurred more in-depth conversations on the cultural dynamics of Hollywood and how problematic characters like Dick Cheney are portrayed there.

In response to Bale's speech, self-identified Satanists and Satanic organizations, notably the Church of Satan, expressed appreciation for the recognition of their belief system in popular culture. While some viewed Bale's remarks as lighthearted, others interpreted them as a nod to the broader influence of Satanism within Hollywood. This reaction highlights the complex relationship between mainstream entertainment and fringe beliefs, where humor can inadvertently blur the lines between satire and genuine endorsement.

Conspiracy theories alleging Hollywood's association with Luciferian practitioners have circulated for decades, fueled by sensationalist narratives and anecdotal evidence. While concrete proof is scarce, these theories often point to perceived occult symbolism in films, rumored rituals among industry insiders, and instances of celebrities making cryptic statements or gestures. Despite lacking empirical validation, these theories persist, fueled by distrust of powerful elites and a fascination with the esoteric.

Luciferian influence extends beyond mere symbolism, with some theorists speculating about its impact on decision-makers within Hollywood. Allegations suggest that powerful industry insiders, driven by esoteric beliefs, manipulate cultural narratives and exert control over creative expression. Comedians, known for their subversive humor and willingness to challenge norms, are often seen as unwitting pawns or willing collaborators in this alleged agenda. However, these claims remain speculative, lacking substantive evidence to support their validity.

Christian Bale's Golden Globes speech is a microcosm of the broader discourse surrounding Hollywood's alleged ties to Luciferian beliefs. While his remarks were meant in jest, they underscore more profound anxieties about the influence of fringe ideologies within mainstream entertainment. This paper illuminates the complexities of belief, power, and cultural production in the entertainment industry by critically examining reactions to Bale's speech and exploring conspiracy theories about Hollywood's occult connections.

Christian Bale's Golden Globes acceptance speech and the ensuing reactions from Satanists and critics shed light on the intricate interplay between belief systems and popular culture. However, while these events spark discussions about Hollywood's potential ties to Luciferian beliefs, assertions about widespread occult influence within the industry should be approached with caution. While conspiracy theories may capture public intrigue, it is crucial to maintain a skeptical perspective and prioritize verifiable evidence when evaluating claims about the influence of fringe ideologies on powerful industry insiders and comedians. By fostering critical inquiry and rational discourse, we can navigate the complexities of belief systems and cultural production in the entertainment industry with greater clarity and understanding.

Satanists' Goal of Wealth and Energy Through Hollywood Luciferian Managers

The alleged objectives of Satan worshipers, particularly those occupying influential positions within industries like Hollywood, are to amass wealth and energy. It investigates the concept of Luciferian managers and handlers who purportedly wield control through blackmail, manipulating, and exerting influence over the entertainment industry. By scrutinizing claims and evidence surrounding the revelation of Luciferian managers' use of blackmail, this paper aims to illuminate the intricate dynamics of power, manipulation, and secrecy within entertainment.

Satan worshipers purportedly seek to amass wealth and energy through various means, including ritualistic practices and manipulation of societal structures. By harnessing dark forces and exploiting vulnerabilities, they allegedly accumulate power, influence, and material wealth, often at the expense of others. The allure of wealth and power has long been associated with individuals in positions of authority, and allegations of Satan worshipers leveraging their influence to accumulate both have persisted, especially within Hollywood.

Luciferian managers are believed to wield significant control over individuals within the entertainment industry, employing tactics such as blackmail to maintain their sway. These managers purportedly manipulate and exploit performers, directors, and other industry insiders, coercing them into compliance through threats of exposure or ruin.

The concept of Luciferian managers sheds light on the shadowy figures behind the scenes who exert influence and control over the careers and lives of those within Hollywood's orbit.

Blackmail is a potent tool in Luciferian managers' arsenal, enabling them to exert control over their targets. By leveraging compromising information or illicit activities, these managers manipulate their subjects, ensuring loyalty and obedience through fear of repercussion or exposure. While concrete evidence supporting claims of Luciferian managers' use of blackmail may be lacking, there have been instances of whistleblowers and insiders shedding light on corruption and abuse within the entertainment industry.

Despite the verification challenges, these revelations underscore the need for scrutiny and accountability within Hollywood's power structures. The alleged pursuit of wealth and energy by Satan worshipers through Luciferian managers in Hollywood remains a contentious topic, fueling speculation and conspiracy theories. While definitive evidence may be elusive, allegations of manipulation, coercion, and blackmail within the entertainment industry raise crucial questions about ethical conduct and power dynamics. As scrutiny persists, the need for transparency and accountability within Hollywood's corridors of influence becomes increasingly evident.

The alleged objectives of Satan worshipers in Hollywood, mainly through the utilization of Luciferian managers and blackmail, reveal a complex web of power, manipulation, and secrecy within the entertainment industry. While definitive evidence may be lacking, the prevalence of allegations underscores the importance of scrutiny and accountability in confronting systemic corruption and abuse. As discussions continue, it is imperative to remain vigilant and uphold principles of transparency and ethical conduct in all facets of the entertainment industry.

Hollywood, often depicted as a beacon of glitz and glamour, harbors a darker side characterized by abuse, exploitation, and corruption. This paper endeavors to uncover these troubling aspects, emphasizing the crucial role of awareness and advocacy in addressing systemic issues within the entertainment industry. By shedding light on Hollywood's dark side, we aim to catalyze positive transformation and promote social justice.

Hollywood's dark side encompasses a myriad of troubling issues, including sexual abuse, harassment, discrimination, and exploitation. While some scandals have garnered public attention, these problems persist throughout the industry, affecting individuals from various backgrounds and positions. The consequences of Hollywood's dark side extend beyond individual suffering, permeating societal norms and industry culture.

Victims of abuse and exploitation in Hollywood endure profound trauma, career setbacks, and psychological distress. Moreover, systemic issues perpetuate inequality, injustice, and the normalization of harmful behaviors, contributing to a toxic culture within the industry and broader society. Understanding the intersectionality of these issues is essential for fostering meaningful change.

Exposing Hollywood's dark side serves multiple crucial purposes. Firstly, it validates and supports survivors, encouraging them to speak out and seek justice. Additionally, raising awareness empowers the public to recognize and challenge harmful practices within the industry, fostering a culture of accountability and ethical responsibility. By shedding light on abusive practices, we can begin to dismantle entrenched power structures and demand systemic change.

Efforts to address Hollywood's dark side require comprehensive advocacy strategies. This may involve challenging industry leaders, advocating for legal and policy reforms, fostering collective action, and promoting cultural shifts prioritizing the safety and well-being of all individuals within the industry. Transparency and accountability are fundamental in this endeavor, ensuring that perpetrators are held accountable and survivors are supported.

Exposing Hollywood's dark side is not merely about sensational revelations but about advocating for justice, empowerment, and positive change. Through awareness-raising efforts, survivor support, and advocacy for systemic reforms, we can work towards transforming Hollywood into a more transparent, accountable, and ethical industry. In this place, creativity thrives without fear of exploitation or harm. By standing together, we can create a brighter future for all those involved in the entertainment industry.

Exposing Hollywood's dark side is essential to promoting awareness and advocating for change within the entertainment industry. We can foster a culture of transparency, accountability, and ethical conduct by confronting systemic abuse, exploitation, and corruption. Together, let us strive for a Hollywood that upholds the dignity and rights of all individuals, ensuring a safer and more equitable environment for everyone involved.

Beneath the entertainment industry's glitz and glamour lies a darker reality of power dynamics and manipulation. This paper delves into the alleged manipulation of artists' careers and earnings by Luciferian handlers within the entertainment industry. By examining the tactics employed and the consequences for artists, this paper seeks to illuminate the darker aspects of power dynamics in Hollywood.

Luciferian handlers wield significant influence within the entertainment industry, controlling artists' careers and earnings through coercion, manipulation, and exploitation. These handlers utilize tactics such as blackmail, threats, and psychological manipulation to maintain control over their clients. They exploit vulnerabilities like financial insecurity or personal struggles to coerce artists into unfavorable contracts, roles, or activities.

Handlers dictate how artists' earnings are managed and distributed, engaging in financial fraud to maximize profits at artists' expense. They use psychological manipulation to groom artists, instill obedience, and suppress dissent, creating dependency and reliance on the handler for guidance. The consequences of manipulation by Luciferian handlers can include loss of autonomy, financial exploitation, mental health issues, and damage to reputation and career prospects.

The manipulation of artists' careers and earnings by Luciferian handlers demands attention, as it perpetuates a culture of exploitation and abuse within the entertainment industry. By shedding light on their tactics and consequences, we can promote industry transparency, accountability, and ethical conduct. Empowering artists to resist manipulation and exploitation is crucial for fostering a safer and more equitable environment for everyone involved.

They are exploring the Quest for the Embodiment of Lucifer's Minions and the Pursuit of Physical Attachment. In religious, mythological, and occult traditions, Lucifer's minions are believed to seek attachment to physical bodies in the earthly realm. This paper explores the motivations behind this quest for embodiment, focusing on the desire to experience sensations and pleasures unique to the physical world. By examining various perspectives, this paper aims to provide insights into Lucifer's minions' mystical and symbolic significance and their pursuit of bodily attachment.

Lucifer's minions are driven by a deep longing to partake in the sensory delights of the physical world, including pleasure, pain, desire, and other earthly experiences. Their motivations may stem from curiosity, rebellion, or a quest for power and control. By seeking embodiment, these entities aim to indulge in earthly pleasures and fulfill their desires, which are inaccessible in their non-corporeal state.

The attachment of Lucifer's minions to physical bodies carries significant implications for both individuals and the broader spiritual realm. It may lead to possession, obsession, or manipulation of human hosts, spiritual warfare, and conflict between forces of light and darkness. Understanding the implications of this attachment is essential for navigating spiritual and metaphysical realms.

The concept of Lucifer's minions seeking attachment to physical bodies for earthly sensations is rooted in various traditions and beliefs. By exploring their motivations and implications, we gain insight into this phenomenon's mystical and symbolic significance. Through awareness, advocacy, and collective action, we can strive to create a culture that prioritizes integrity and spiritual well-being, safeguarding individuals from manipulation and exploitation.

Exploring Ritual Abuse Allegations Against Transient Youth

Allegations of rituals involving transient youth, especially those heavily drugged or vulnerable, evoke profound concern and demand meticulous scrutiny of society's darker corners. While sporadic reports surface, it is imperative to approach these claims cautiously, relying on verified evidence rather than succumbing to sensationalism. This paper delves into the troubling trend of transient youth being targeted for alleged involvement in rituals, highlighting the complexities involved and underscoring the critical need to safeguard vulnerable populations.

Transient or homeless youth confront daunting challenges, including poverty, abuse, and neglect, rendering them highly susceptible to exploitation. Their lack of stable support systems makes them prime targets for predatory individuals or groups seeking to capitalize on their vulnerabilities.

Reports indicate that predators, including human traffickers and individuals engaged in illicit activities, actively prey on transient youth for nefarious purposes, ranging from sexual exploitation to forced labor.

Exploiting the isolation and desperation of transient youth, predators dangle false promises of safety, belonging, or material rewards to trap them in difficult situations, perpetuating cycles of abuse and victimization.

Rituals Involving Vulnerable Youth: Allegations of Ritual Abuse: Over the years, sporadic allegations of rituals involving vulnerable youth, mainly those heavily drugged, have emerged. These allegations often include disturbing accounts of Satanic or occult rituals, sexual abuse, torture, and even human sacrifice.

Verifying such allegations presents formidable challenges due to the clandestine nature of these activities and the compromised state of the victims involved. Victims, especially heavily drugged transient youth, may struggle to recall or articulate their experiences, complicating efforts to gather reliable evidence.

Investigating allegations of ritual abuse demands coordinated efforts among law enforcement agencies, social services, and victim support organizations. Prosecuting perpetrators and providing comprehensive support to victims, particularly among marginalized or transient populations, requires navigating intricate legal and investigative hurdles.

Heightened awareness of the vulnerabilities faced by transient youth and education on indicators of exploitation and abuse are critical preventive measures. Empowering communities to recognize and report suspicious activities can serve as a shield against harm for transient youth.

Support Services: Establishing robust support services, including shelter, counseling, and access to education and employment opportunities, is paramount in safeguarding transient youth. Providing pathways to stability and empowerment can deter them from falling prey to predators.

Fostering collaboration among law enforcement agencies, social services, community organizations, and advocacy groups is essential in identifying and addressing instances of exploitation and abuse involving transient youth. By pooling resources and expertise, stakeholders can work synergistically to protect vulnerable populations.

While allegations of rituals involving transient youth stir profound concern, navigating these complex issues demands circumspection and diligence. Collaborative efforts to raise awareness, provide support services, and investigate allegations are pivotal in safeguarding vulnerable populations and upholding their rights and dignity. As we confront these challenges, let us remain vigilant, prioritizing the safety and well-being of transient youth amidst the intricate tapestry of societal complexities.

Allegations of Satan worship and blood sacrifices among individuals in positions of power, particularly within industries like Hollywood, have ignited controversy and intrigue in recent years. This paper delves into the claims of worshippers engaging in dark practices concealed beneath a veneer of respectability, aiming to shed light on a shadowy aspect of society and provoke thoughtful inquiry into the influence of occult beliefs on individuals in positions of authority.

Conspiracy theories alleging the presence of Satan worshippers in Hollywood and other influential spheres challenge conventional perceptions of power and prestige. These theories suggest that behind the glamorous façade of fame and fortune lies a darker reality, where individuals engage in rituals involving the worship of Satan and sinister sacrifices. Moreover, proponents of these theories argue that these practices are not merely for personal gratification but also the accumulation of wealth and energy through occult rituals.

While such claims often lack tangible evidence, proponents point to alleged symbolism in media, cryptic statements from insiders, and occasional whistleblowers as supporting factors. The veil of respectability these individuals maintain adds to the intrigue, as their public personas often convey success, talent, and philanthropy. However, according to conspiracy theorists, behind closed doors, these same individuals partake in rituals that involve offering sacrifices to dark forces.

The concept of blood sacrifices, while disturbing, aligns with historical associations of occult practices with ritualistic offerings. Critics caution against jumping to conclusions, citing the lack of concrete evidence and the potential for misinformation and sensationalism in conspiracy narratives.

Beyond the macabre rituals, proponents argue that the ultimate goal of these worshippers is not merely personal enrichment but also the accumulation of wealth and energy through their dark practices. By engaging in rituals purportedly tapping into supernatural energies, these worshippers seek to enhance their success, control, and longevity.

However, skepticism abounds, with critics highlighting the lack of verifiable evidence and the potential for moral panic and witch hunts. The danger of demonizing individuals based on unsubstantiated claims underscores the importance of discernment and critical thinking.

Moreover, attributing complex social phenomena solely to occult beliefs overlooks systemic issues such as inequality, exploitation, and abuse of power. While conspiracy theories may offer a simplistic narrative to explain perceived injustices, they risk obscuring deeper structural problems and undermining efforts to address them.

The presence of alleged Satan worshippers in positions of power raises profound questions about the intersection of belief, influence, and morality in contemporary society. While claims of dark practices provoke both fascination and alarm, it's essential to approach these assertions with caution, skepticism, and a commitment to evidence-based inquiry. By critically examining the evidence and engaging in reasoned discourse, we can navigate the complexities of these allegations while upholding principles of justice, accountability, and human dignity.

The presence of alleged Satan worshipers in positions of power, particularly within industries like Hollywood, has sparked controversy, speculation, and a labyrinth of conspiracy theories. Allegations of individuals engaging in Satanic rituals and blood sacrifices have circulated for years, prompting scrutiny into the intersection of belief systems, power dynamics, and evil influences in authority. This paper delves into these allegations, explores the concept of concealed evil, and seeks to unravel the complexities surrounding the alleged presence of Satan worshipers in positions of influence. By examining evidence, testimonies, and societal implications, this paper aims to shed light on the nuanced dynamics within the entertainment industry.

The entertainment industry, especially Hollywood, has long been a focal point for rumors and conspiracy theories regarding Satan worship and occult practices. Allegations of prominent figures engaging in rituals involving blood sacrifices have persisted, raising questions about the true nature of power and influence in society. This paper explores these allegations, examining the concept of concealed evil and its implications for belief systems and power dynamics.

The entertainment industry has been rife with allegations of individuals participating in Satan worship and occult rituals. Claims range from high-profile celebrities allegedly engaging in blood sacrifices to rumors of secret Satanic cults operating within Hollywood's elite circles. While concrete evidence may be scarce, the prevalence of such allegations has fueled speculation and conspiracy theories, leading to heightened public interest in the topic.

One intriguing aspect of the presence of alleged Satan worshipers in positions of power is the notion of concealed evil. Some individuals may use the guise of Satan worship to hide their true intentions and manipulate others for personal gain. By presenting themselves as followers of dark forces, these individuals may exert control and influence over others, exploiting fear and awe to further their agendas.

The intersection of belief systems and power dynamics within Hollywood is complex and multifaceted. While some individuals may genuinely adhere to Satanic beliefs and rituals, others may exploit the symbolism and imagery associated with Satanism for their ends. Understanding the motivations and intentions behind these actions requires careful examination of individual behaviors, societal norms, and cultural influences.

Separating fact from fiction in allegations of Satan worship and blood sacrifices in Hollywood is a daunting task. While there may be instances of individuals engaging in occult practices, attributing such actions to a widespread conspiracy of Satan worshipers necessitates verifiable evidence. By critically analyzing claims, scrutinizing testimonies, and corroborating evidence, we can endeavor to unveil the truth behind these allegations and discern the realities of influence and authority within the entertainment industry.

The allegations of Satan worshipers in positions of power, particularly within Hollywood, remain a topic of intrigue and debate. Claims of individuals engaging in occult practices and blood sacrifices prompt reflection on belief systems, power dynamics, and the nature of concealed evil. By critically examining evidence and testimonies, we can strive to unravel the complexities surrounding these allegations and gain insights into the dynamics of influence and authority within society's most influential circles.

Uncovering the Tragic Phenomenon of Missing and Exploited Homeless Individuals

Homelessness is a pervasive social issue that affects millions worldwide, with individuals experiencing homelessness often vulnerable to exploitation and violence. This paper sheds light on the disturbing phenomenon of homeless people going missing and becoming victims of exploitation, including cases where they are targeted for nefarious purposes such as human trafficking or ritualistic sacrifice. Through examining case studies, statistical data, and relevant literature, this paper explores the root causes and systemic failures that contribute to the vulnerability of homeless individuals and the urgent need for comprehensive solutions to address this humanitarian crisis.

Homelessness is a multifaceted problem that extends beyond the lack of adequate housing, encompassing issues of poverty, mental illness, and social marginalization. In recent years, reports of homeless individuals disappearing under suspicious circumstances have raised concerns about the exploitation and victimization of this already vulnerable population. This paper aims to investigate the unsettling phenomenon of homeless people going missing and becoming targets of exploitation and sacrifice.

Homeless individuals face a myriad of challenges that render them particularly susceptible to exploitation and violence. Factors such as restricted access to resources, a lack of social support networks, and stigma increase their vulnerability and make them accessible targets for predators. Many homeless persons struggle with mental health issues or drug addiction, which enhances their vulnerability and likelihood of falling victim to exploitation.

Numerous cases have emerged where homeless individuals have gone missing under suspicious circumstances, with some believed to have been abducted or lured into dangerous situations. These cases often receive minimal attention from law enforcement and the media, exacerbating the invisibility and marginalization of homeless populations. Furthermore, the transient nature of homelessness can make it challenging to track and investigate cases of missing individuals, further hindering efforts to address this issue.

Homeless individuals are frequently targeted for exploitation, including forced labor, sexual exploitation, and human trafficking. Traffickers prey on the vulnerabilities of homeless individuals, exploiting their desperate circumstances for profit. Moreover, homeless youth are particularly at risk, with many falling victim to exploitation and trafficking networks that operate both domestically and internationally.

In addition to exploitation and trafficking, there have been unsubstantiated reports and urban legends suggesting that homeless individuals are targeted for ritualistic sacrifice or occult practices. While such claims often lack credible evidence, they underscore the profound vulnerability and marginalization experienced by homeless populations, as well as the prevalence of sensationalism and stigma surrounding homelessness.

To adequately address the issue of missing and exploited homeless persons, it is necessary to address the core causes of homelessness, including a lack of affordable housing and inadequate social support services. Comprehensive strategies that prioritize housing stability, access to mental health services, and employment opportunities are critical for addressing the vulnerabilities that make homeless individuals targets for exploitation.

The phenomenon of homeless people going missing and becoming victims of exploitation and sacrifice is a tragic manifestation of the systemic failures and societal neglect that perpetuate homelessness. Urgent action is necessary to address the root causes of homelessness and develop comprehensive solutions that prioritize the safety and well-being of people experiencing homelessness. By raising awareness and fighting for significant change, we may contribute to a future where no one is left behind or forgotten on the streets.

San Francisco residents are in uproar because homeless people are disappearing. If you do any investigation, you will be surprised at how many individuals have gone missing and how the talk was to stay out of the shelters and missions. In New York City, there is a new monument portraying a reptile abducting a kid with a sack over their head. Things are not concealed; they are seen.

Halloween is the number one time of year when most humans sacrifice for the devil on the planet. I know some people say this sounds ridiculous because it's about candy and costumes, but it's also the number one week when homeless people go missing. Unmarked vans go around and offer to pick up people experiencing homelessness and take them to shelters or places for free meals; then they bind them, keep them, and sacrifice them on Halloween. In Thailand, different people buy a spot with cryptocurrency in a red room, so they can't be traced. Where a child is murdered every three weeks, and the person who pays with the crypto gets to choose how that kid is murdered, and the other person gets to do things with them. This is trafficking murder, rape, and trafficking. The scary thing was Not only in Thailand. During raids in multiple countries, they discovered shipping containers converted into individual torture chambers, all outfitted with cameras and studio lighting. One girl was found and had been kept in a container for two months; her abductor admitted to killing over a dozen women after using them for his torture stream. People pay a lot of money for this service, using code words to describe the type of torture they want to witness. Law enforcement believes there are many more places and hopes to uncover the missing folks trapped in a crimson chamber. The disappearing homeless vehicles scooping up people and recording murder and torture is not a new phenomenon. David and I were studying the Atlanta child murders, the Son of Sam, and other lesser-known incidents involving abductions, vans, and snuff videos.

A Call to Action for Collective Resolve

The harrowing realities of child sex trafficking persist as a dark stain on our society, preying upon the innocence of our children and inflicting unimaginable harm. In confronting this sobering reality, it becomes evident that protecting our children from exploitation is not just a moral imperative but a fundamental duty that transcends all other considerations. This paper serves as a clarion call for collective action to end child sex trafficking, shedding light on its pervasive evil and urging society to confront this heinous crime with courage, compassion, and unwavering resolve.

Child sex trafficking represents a pervasive evil that thrives in the shadows, exploiting the vulnerability of innocent children for profit and pleasure. Its dark realities are characterized by exploitation, abuse, and the violation of fundamental human rights. Despite efforts to combat it, child sex trafficking continues to cast a long and sinister shadow over our society, necessitating urgent and concerted action.

Ending child sex trafficking is not merely a moral imperative; it is a shared responsibility that transcends political, social, and cultural divides. As individuals and as a society, we bear a collective obligation to protect our children from exploitation and abuse, regardless of our roles or affiliations. It is only through unified and coordinated efforts that we can effectively dismantle the networks of trafficking and bring justice to the victims.

Confronting child sex trafficking requires courage as we shine a light into the darkest corners of human depravity and hold perpetrators accountable for their crimes. It demands a compassionate response, recognizing the profound trauma and suffering endured by victims and survivors. Only by addressing the root causes of vulnerability and providing comprehensive support to survivors can we honestly confront the darkness and pave the way for healing and justice.

Confronting child sex trafficking demands unwavering resolve as we mobilize resources, implement evidence-based strategies, and strengthen legal protections for victims. It requires a long-term commitment to dismantling trafficking networks, disrupting supply chains, and addressing the systemic factors that perpetuate vulnerability. Ending child sex trafficking will not be easy. Still, with determination and persistence, we can achieve tangible progress toward a future where every child is safe, cherished, and free from exploitation and abuse.

Child sex trafficking remains a grave injustice that demands our collective attention and action. As we confront the sobering reality of this pervasive crime, let us reaffirm our commitment to protecting the innocence of our children. We can work toward a future where every child is safe, cherished, and free to pursue their dreams through collective action, unwavering commitment, and steadfast advocacy. Together, let us stand united against child sex trafficking and strive to create a world where our children can thrive in safety and dignity.

As we conclude this journey through the shadows and complexities of our world, I extend my deepest gratitude to you, the reader, for accompanying me on this exploration. Together, we have delved into the depths of darkness, confronting unsettling truths and uncovering uncomfortable realities. Through our collective inquiry, we have sought to shed light on the obscured corners of society, challenging assumptions and inspiring action.

The revelations presented in these pages are not merely anecdotes or conjectures; they reflect the profound challenges we face as a global community. From the insidious grip of child sex trafficking to the disturbing allegations of Satanism and corruption in Hollywood, each topic we have examined serves as a stark reminder of the enduring struggle for justice, integrity, and compassion.

Yet, amidst the darkness, there is also hope. With each call to action and commitment to change, we reaffirm our shared humanity and collective resolve to create a better world. By amplifying the voices of survivors, advocating for justice, and demanding accountability from those in power, we take meaningful steps toward dismantling systems of exploitation and oppression.

As you close these pages and reflect on our journey, I invite you to consider the impact of our collective efforts. Whether you have been stirred to action, inspired to learn more, or moved by the stories shared within these pages, your engagement in this discourse is a testament to the power of knowledge, empathy, and solidarity.

May this book catalyze continued inquiry, dialogue, and action. May it inspire you to seek truth, challenge injustice, and stand in solidarity with those who have been marginalized and oppressed. May it remind you that, even in the darkest times, there is always a glimmer of light—a beacon of hope guiding us toward a future where every child is safe, every victim is heard, and every voice is valued.

In the depths where shadows fall,
Whispers echo through the hall,
Secrets kept from light of day,
In hidden corners they will stay.
Revelations shrouded in black,
Truths obscured, no turning back,
Mysteries veiled in darkened guise,
Unraveling beneath the skies.
Whispers murmur, secrets keep,
In the shadows, dark and deep,
Whispers of the hidden past,
Revealing shadows that will last.
In the darkness, truths unfold,
Stories waiting to be told,
From the shadows, secrets rise,

Unveiling truth before our eyes.
So listen closely, if you dare,
To secrets whispered in the air,
For in the shadows, deep and wide,
Revelations do reside.

Thank you for embarking on this journey with me. May our collective efforts pave the way for a more just, compassionate, and equitable world for future generations.

With deepest gratitude and hope,

Printed in the United States
by Baker & Taylor Publisher Services